CW01283393

Simplified Morning and Evening Prayer

Fuller forms of Morning and Evening Prayer
available from HarperCollins*Publishers:*

Shorter Morning and Evening Prayer
Morning and Evening Prayer
The Divine Office Vol. I (Advent to Lent)
The Divine Office Vol. II (Ash Wednesday to Pentecost)
The Divine Office Vol. III (Weeks 6–34 of the Year)

SIMPLIFIED MORNING AND EVENING PRAYER

AN INTRODUCTION TO THE DIVINE OFFICE

Edited and with an introduction by John Brook

HarperCollins*Publishers*

HarperCollins*Publishers*
77–85 Fulham Palace Road, London W6 8JB

First published in Great Britain
in 1997 by HarperCollins*Publishers*

1 3 5 7 9 10 8 6 4 2

Taken from *The Divine Office*, a translation of *Liturgia Horarum*,
approved by the Episcopal Conferences of Australia, England and
Wales, Ireland, Scotland.

Also approved for use in Gambia, Ghana, India, Kenya, Liberia,
Malaysia and Singapore, New Zealand, Nigeria, Zimbabwe,
Sierra Leone, Tanzania, Uganda.

The Divine Office, © 1974, the hierarchies of Australia, England and
Wales, Ireland. Original English version of intercessions, concluding
prayers, antiphons, short responses, responsories, © 1974, the
hierarchies of Australia, England and Wales, Ireland.

Copyright © 1997 Compilation of this excerpt from *The Divine
Office* and editorial matter, HarperCollins*Publishers*

A catalogue record for this book is available
from the British Library

0 00 599374 1

Printed and bound in Great Britain by
Caledonian International Book Manufacturing Ltd, Glasgow

CONDITIONS OF SALE

This book is sold subject to the condition that it shall not, by way of
trade or otherwise, be lent, resold, hired out or otherwise circulated
without the publisher's prior consent in any form of binding or cover
other than that in which it is published and without a similar condition
including this condition being imposed on the subsequent purchaser.

All rights reserved. No part of this publication may be reproduced,
stored in a retrieval system, or transmitted in any form or by any means,
electronic, mechanical, photocopying, recording or otherwise, without
the prior permission of the publishers.

NIHIL OBSTAT:
Rev. Anton Cowan, Censor

IMPRIMATUR:
Monsignor Ralph Brown, Vicar General
Westminster, 5th day of February 1997

The Nihil obstat and Imprimatur are a declaration that a book or pamphlet is considered to be free from doctrinal or moral error. It is not implied that those who have granted the Nihil obstat and Imprimatur agree with the contents, opinions or statements expressed.

Contents

Acknowledgements IX
Introduction XI

Week 1		*Week 3*	
Sunday	1	Sunday	77
Monday	6	Monday	82
Tuesday	11	Tuesday	87
Wednesday	17	Wednesday	92
Thursday	22	Thursday	97
Friday	27	Friday	102
Saturday	33	Saturday	108
Week 2		*Week 4*	
Sunday	38	Sunday	114
Monday	44	Monday	121
Tuesday	50	Tuesday	127
Wednesday	56	Wednesday	133
Thursday	62	Thursday	139
Friday	66	Friday	144
Saturday	72	Saturday	150

The Lord's Prayer 156

Acknowledgements

The Publishers are grateful to the following for permission to reproduce copyright material:

SCRIPTURE TEXTS

The following versions have been used:
Knox Bible, © 1945, 1949, the Hierarchy of England and Wales.
New English Bible, 2nd edition copyright 1970, Oxford and Cambridge University Presses.
Revised Standard Version, Common Bible, copyrighted © 1973, by the Division of Christian Education, National Council of the Churches of Christ in the USA. Special permission has been obtained to use in this publication the 'you-your-yours' forms of the personal pronoun in the address to God.
Today's English Version (*Good News for Modern Man*), United Bible Societies of America and Collins Publishers, London.
Psalm texts are translated from the Hebrew by The Grail, © The Grail (England) 1963, and published by Collins. They are reprinted from the Singing Version first published by Fontana Books in 1966.
The practical needs of choral recitation prompted a number of revisions in the psalms and canticles of this Breviary. These revisions are made with the agreement of The Grail.

ACKNOWLEDGEMENTS

SCRIPTURE VERSIONS USED FOR CANTICLES

GRAIL VERSION
1 Samuel 2:1–10
Isaiah 12:1–6
Daniel 3:52–57
Hab 3:2–4, 13a, 15–19
Luke 1:68–79

REVISED STANDARD VERSION
1 Chron 29:10–13
Isaiah 26:1–4, 7–9, 12; 40:10–17
Ezekiel 36:24–28
Ephesians 1:3–10
Philippians 2:6–11
Colossians 1:12–20
Revelation 4:11; 5:9, 10, 12; 11:17–18; 12:10b–12a; 15:3–4

For a fuller introduction to the Divine Office, including suggestions on how to pray the psalms, see *The School of Prayer: An Introduction to the Divine Office for all Christians*, John Brook, HarperCollins, 1992.

Introduction

This book is a simplified version of the Morning and Evening Prayer that is found in the Divine Office. It is designed specifically for ordinary Christians who want to have a more regular structure to their prayer but perhaps are unsure where to begin. It allows use firstly for individual prayer, although there is no reason why this form cannot be used in a group.

Prayer and the Bible have long been inexorably linked. If we are to come to know God revealed in Christ, we must come to know the Scriptures. St John says of the words of his Gospel: 'These are written that you may believe that Jesus is the Christ, the Son of God, and that believing you may have life in his name.' (John 20:31) The Divine Office – and hence the prayer sections in this book – is a priceless gift, in giving a daily diet from the Bible for the purpose of meditation and prayer.

We learn to pray by taking the prayers inspired by the Holy Spirit and copying them. As we take these prayers and copy them, with concentration of mind and heart, the same Spirit who inspired them will inspire us to pray. The Office resolves the difficulty of finding words. It helps focus distractions and enlarges vision. Regular prayer in the morning and evening is the way which Jesus himself learned to pray, according to his Jewish customs.

Some may never have prayed the Divine Office before, others may have tried and given up because it seemed too complicated. Many lay people who have not used the psalms in prayer before find the full diet of prayer in the Divine Office more than they can handle. The full text presents a bewildering variety of Scripture. This version is designed to give a genuine flavour of the full text, but in doses small enough to prevent giving indigestion.

INTRODUCTION

However, it is not intended to replace fuller forms of Morning and Evening Prayer which make up the Divine Office. Rather it can become a stepping stone. After using the simplified form for a number of months, perhaps even for a year or more, it should be easier to move on to the full form.

In most cases, the psalms for each day in this simplified form are those from Morning and Evening Prayer for the same day. The most straightforward psalms and canticles have been selected for each day. The Scripture reading and intercessions are always those set down for that day in the Office.

This simplified version takes the following form:

- A four week cycle of Morning and Evening Prayer.
- Each day's Morning and Evening Prayer consists of a psalm (and sometimes a canticle), a short Bible reading and intercessory prayers, and ends with a recital of the Lord's Prayer.

GETTING STARTED

The advantage with this simplified form of Morning and Evening Prayer is that it allows you to start slowly. The most important thing is not to try too much and so become discouraged and give up. Move along at your own pace. The following suggestions may help:

1. Choose a time for prayer that fits in with your daily routine. If you are working outside the home, you may find time while you commute to or from work. It may be necessary to adjust your daily routines to make time for prayer, by getting up earlier. Whatever time you choose, it will take discipline and perseverance to stick to it.
2. Find a place where you can be quiet and still. It may be helpful to set a small table, with a cloth, a candle and a cross.

INTRODUCTION

3. Read each psalm slowly and seek to enter into the heart of the psalm, into the experience it comes out of. You will find your own prayer emerging out of the prayer of the psalmist. If you wish, pause for personal prayer or reflection between each section.
4. Read the Scripture reading as the word of God addressed to you for that day.
5. In the intercessions bring your own needs and the needs of others to the Lord, guided by the intercessions given for each day. You may wish to add intercessory prayers of your own after the suggested prayers. Pray with confidence and faith.
6. The Lord's Prayer sums up the whole experience of Christian prayer. One of the Church's greatest teachers on prayer, St Teresa of Avila said: 'Whoever prays the Lord's Prayer with complete attention and devotion of heart rises to the heights of prayer.'

Remember that the Divine Office is also a community prayer. Some churches gather together for Evening Prayer on Sundays. Some religious communities welcome others to pray the Office with them. If you know of someone else who prays the Office or wants to, pray together if you can.

If you are praying in a group, you may wish to alternate verses of the psalm and the responses amongst members. This may involve a leader speaking first and the group responding, or having the group split into two parts.

THE DIVINE OFFICE

This pattern of prayer is one of the Christian Church's greatest treasures of prayer. The word 'Office' comes from the Latin *officium*, meaning 'service', 'something done for someone'. The Office is also called the Liturgy of the Hours, referring to the

INTRODUCTION

seven 'hours', or times of prayer for each day. It is part of the public liturgy of the Church.

The Divine Office is a pattern of prayer based on the Bible, in particular the psalms. In the early centuries of the Christian Church, the Office was the prayer of the whole Christian community, not just the clergy. By medieval times the Office had, outside the monasteries, become the private prayer of the clergy. The Second Vatican Council of the Catholic Church revised the Office in such a way as to restore it to its original function as the prayer of the whole people of God. Morning and Evening Prayer are 'the two hinges on which the daily office turns', said the Council.

In fact, the regular cycle of prayer in the Office has found new devotees among Christians of many backgrounds. Its respectful use of the Scriptures appeals to the deepest convictions of Protestant as well as Catholic Christians. It is natural that Protestants may have reservations about using a traditionally Catholic form of prayer, but this form can be commended to all. The Office brings Bible passages alive for all those of faith seeking to bring its riches into their regular prayer.

THE FORM OF SIMPLIFIED MORNING AND EVENING PRAYER

I PSALMODY, OR PSALTER

'Psalmody' means 'a collection of psalms arranged for singing'. 'Psalter' can refer to the Book of Psalms, or to a book of psalms arranged for liturgical use. When used of the Office both words refer to the collection of psalms arranged for prayer.

The psalms for Morning and Evening Prayer have been carefully selected and arranged to best aid Christian worship. The psalmody of Morning Prayer consists of psalms whose mood and content fit the beginning of the day. Often the psalm will be a psalm of praise which lifts our minds to God and to his glory, and puts our own lives in their proper perspective.

The psalm may be followed by a canticle. A canticle is a song, a hymn of praise, a psalm which comes from somewhere else in Scripture other than the Book of Psalms. At Morning Prayer the canticle is always from the Old Testament and is often a classic passage from the prophets, especially Isaiah.

The psalmody of Evening Prayer consists of psalms chosen because of the way they express prayer at the end of the day. If there is a canticle it will be from the New Testament (from the Epistles or Revelation). The dominant note of the evening psalms is thanksgiving. In the evening we give thanks to God for the gift of the day.

The version of the psalms used in the Office is the Grail version, a translation designed especially for liturgical use. It is a translation which captures the poetry of the Hebrew original, and expresses the meaning in clear English. It is an excellent version because it has a simplicity and flow which make it a great aid to praying the psalms.

The numbering of the psalms in the Office is different from the numbering in most versions of the Bible. The Office preserves the numbering system followed by the early Church, which used the Greek and Latin translations of the Hebrew text. The Greek (Septuagint) and Latin (Vulgate) versions join the Hebrew Psalms 9 and 10 together, and join Psalms 114 and 115 together, but divide Psalms 116 and 147 in two. The result is that for most of Psalms 10 to 148 the numbering in the Office is one behind that of a modern translation of the Bible. That is why most psalms in the Office have two numbers. The first number is the liturgical number, following the Greek and Latin versions. The second, in brackets, is the number of the psalm in any modern Bible.

The psalms in the Office are accented for singing and chanting, hence the accent mark ´ over certain words. These are necessary for the antiphonal chanting of the psalms in community, but can be ignored for individual prayer.

INTRODUCTION

Each psalm has an antiphon adapted from a verse in the psalm and designed to highlight a dominant theme in the psalm. The antiphon is said at the beginning of the psalm, or sometimes after each verse.

At the conclusion of each psalm, before the final antiphon, the ascription of praise is often used:

Glory be to the Father and to the Son and to the Holy Spirit, as it was in the beginning is now and ever shall be, world without end. Amen.

2 SCRIPTURE READING

A short reading is given according to the liturgical day, season, or feast. The readings have been chosen with the purpose of expressing succinctly an important biblical theme. At Morning Prayer the reading is usually from the Old Testament. In the evening, it is always from the New Testament.

The Scripture readings can be prayed following the pattern of what St Benedict called *lectio divina*, 'sacred reading'. *Lectio divina* has four steps (1) Read the passage. (2) When a word or phrase strikes you, stop reading and meditate on the phrase, allowing it to speak to you, to take root in you. (3) Turn the meditation into brief prayer. (4) *Contemplate* the Lord: be still in God's presence. Then continue reading and repeat the cycle.

3 SILENCE

The silence following the psalms and readings is an integral part of the prayer. In any attentive conversation between friends, after our friend has spoken we often pause, to absorb what they have said before we reply. To pause, to be silent after each psalm, allows the word of God to germinate in us. It gives us time to meditate on the word of God, and to listen to the voice of the Spirit in our hearts.

INTRODUCTION

4 THE RESPONSE

The short verse and response is another way of absorbing the word of God by putting into words a proper response to the Scripture reading. The response is designed to turn the reading into prayer and contemplation. Although it is designed for corporate prayer, the response has great value in individual prayer, because it encourages our careful listening to God's word.

5 THE INTERCESSIONS

The letter to Timothy advises that 'there should be prayers offered for everyone – petitions, intercessions and thanksgiving ... To do this is right, and will please God our Saviour, who wants everyone to be saved and reach full knowledge of the truth' (1 Timothy 2:1–4).

In the morning the intercessions are designed to consecrate the day and our work to God. In the evening, the intercessions focus on the needs of the world. When praying alone, each intercession offers direction for our own personal prayer, bringing before the Lord our specific needs and the needs of those who are known to us. The final intercession each evening is always for the departed.

The intercessions of the Office are a constant stimulus to us to form our own intercessions, to bring to God the needs we carry in our own hearts, and to enlarge our hearts to pray for the needs of the world. The wording of the intercessions in the Office can seem a little vague, but that is because it is designed to be universal, and it is precisely that universal quality which opens our horizons in prayer. We can add our specific prayers at any point in the intercessions.

6 THE LORD'S PRAYER

The Lord's Prayer has place of honour at the end of the intercessions and it sums up the whole prayer.

St Cyprian, a third century Bishop of Carthage, in his treatise *On the Lord's Prayer*, said: 'Let us pray as our God and Master himself taught us. Our prayer is friendly and intimate when we petition God with his own prayer, letting the words of Christ rise to the Father's ears. When we pray, may the Father recognize his Son's own words. He who dwells in our breast should also be our voice.'

Week I: Sunday

MORNING PRAYER

PSALMODY
Ant. 1: To yóu, O God, I keep vigil at dawn to look upon your power, alleluia.

A soul thirsting for God   Psalm 62(63):2–9

Let the man who has put away the deeds of the night watch for God

O Gód, you are my Gód, for you I lóng;
for yóu my sóul is thírsting.
My bódy pínes for yóu
like a drý, weary lánd without wáter.
So I gáze on yóu in the sánctuary
to sée your stréngth and your glóry.

For your lóve is bétter than lífe,
my líps will spéak your práise.
So I will bléss you áll my lífe,
in your náme I will líft up my hánds.
My sóul shall be fílled as with a bánquet,
my móuth shall práise you with jóy.

On my béd I remémber yóu.
On yóu I múse through the níght
for yóu have béen my hélp;
in the shádow of your wings I rejóice.
My sóul clíngs to yóu;
your ríght hand hólds me fást.

WEEK I: SUNDAY

Ant. To you, O God, I keep vigil at dawn, to look upon your power, alleluia.
Ant. 2: Lord our God, we praise the splendour of your name.

To God alone be honour and glory

Canticle: 1 Chron 29:10–13

Blessed be the God and Father of our Lord Jesus Christ

(Eph 1:3)

> Blessed are you, O Lord,
> the God of Israel our father,
> for ever and ever.
>
> Yours, O Lord, is the greatness, and the power,
> and the glory, and the victory, and the majesty;
> for all that is in the heavens and in the earth is yours;
> Yours is the kingdom, O Lord,
> and you are exalted as head above all.
>
> Both riches and honour come from you,
> and you rule over all.
> In your hand are power and might;
> and in your hand it is to make great and to give strength
>   to all.
>
> And now we thank you, our God,
> and praise your glorious name.

Ant. Lord our God, we praise the splendour of your name.

SCRIPTURE READING   Rev 7:10, 12
Victory to our God, who sits on the throne, and to the Lamb! Praise and glory and wisdom and thanksgiving and honour and power and strength to our God for ever and ever. Amen.

WEEK I: SUNDAY

SHORT RESPONSORY

℟ You are the Christ, the Son of the living God. Have mercy on us.

℣ You are seated at the right hand of the Father.

INTERCESSIONS

Let us pray to Christ the Lord, the sun who enlightens all men, whose light will never fail us: ℟ Lord our Saviour, give us life!
Lord of the sun and the stars, we thank you for the gift of a new day; – and we celebrate the day of resurrection. ℟
Lead us by your Spirit to do your will; – guide and protect us by your wisdom. ℟
Bring us to share with joy this Sunday's eucharist; – nourish us by your word, and by your body. ℟
Lord, grant us your gifts, though we are unworthy; – with all our hearts we thank you. ℟
Our Father

EVENING PRAYER

PSALMODY

Ant. O Lord, you will show me the fulness of joy in your presence, alleluia.

The Lord is my portion Psalm 15 (16)

God raised up Jesus, freeing him from the pains of death (Acts 2:24)

Presérve me, Gód, I take réfuge in yóu.
I sáy to the Lórd: 'Yóu are my Gód.
My háppiness líes in yóu alóne.'

He has pút into my héart a márvellous lóve
for the fáithful ónes who dwéll in his lánd.

WEEK I: SUNDAY

Those who chóose other góds incréase their sórrows.
Néver will I óffer their ófferings of blóod.
Néver will I táke their náme upon my líps.

O Lórd, it is yóu who are my pórtion and cúp;
it is yóu yoursélf who áre my prize.
The lót marked óut for me is mý delíght:
welcome indéed the héritage that fálls to mé!

I will bléss the Lórd who gíves me cóunsel,
who éven at níght dirécts my héart,
I kéep the Lórd ever ín my síght:
since hé is at my ríght hand, I shall stand fírm.

And so my héart rejoíces, my sóul is glád;
éven my bódy shall rést in sáfety.
For yóu will not léave my sóul among the déad,
nor lét your belóved knów decáy.

You will shów me the páth of lífe,
the fúlness of jóy in your présence,
at your ríght hand háppiness for éver.

Ant. O Lord, you will show me the fulness of joy in your presence, alleluia.

SCRIPTURE READING 2 Cor 1:3–4
Let us give thanks to the God and Father of our Lord Jesus Christ, the merciful Father, the God from whom all help comes! He helps us in all our troubles, so that we are able to help those who have all kinds of troubles, using the same help that we ourselves have received from God.

SHORT RESPONSORY
℟ Blessed are you, O Lord, in the vault of heaven.
℣ You are exalted and glorified above all else for ever.

INTERCESSIONS

Christ is the Head of his body, the Church, and we are the members of that body; gathered this evening to pray in his name, we say: ℟ Your kingdom come!

May your Church be a light to the nations, the sign and source of your power to unite all men: – may she lead mankind to the mystery of your love. ℟

Guide the Pope and all the bishops of your Church: – grant them the gifts of unity, of love, and of peace. ℟

Lord, give peace to our troubled world; – and give to your children security of mind and freedom from anxiety. ℟

Help us to bring your compassion to the poor, the sick, the lonely, the unloved; – lead us to find you in the coming week. ℟

Awaken the dead to a glorious resurrection: – may we be united with them at the end of time. ℟

Our Father

Week 1: Monday

MORNING PRAYER

PSALMODY
Ant. It is you whom I invoke, O Lord. In the morning you hear me.

Morning prayer for help Psalm 5:2–10, 12–13

Those who have received the Word of God which dwells within will rejoice for ever

To my wórds give éar, O Lórd,
give héed to my gróaning.
Atténd to the sóund of my críes,
my Kíng and my Gód.

It is yóu whom I invóke, O Lórd.
In the mórning, you héar me;
In the mórning I óffer you my práyer,
wátching and wáiting.

Yóu are no Gód who loves évil;
no sínner is your guést.
The bóastful shall not stánd their gróund
befóre your fáce.

You háte áll who do évil;
you destróy all who líe.
The decéitful and blóodthirsty mán
the Lórd detésts.

But I through the gréatness of your lóve
have áccess to your hóuse.

I bów down befóre your holy témple,
fílled with áwe.

Léad me, Lórd, in your jústice,
because of thóse who lie in wáit;
make cléar your way befóre me.

No trúth can be fóund in their móuths,
their héart is all míschief,
their thróat a wíde-open gráve,
all hóney their spéech.

All thóse you protéct shall be glád
and ríng out their jóy.
You shélter them; in yóu they rejóice,
those who lóve your náme.

It is yóu who bless the júst man, Lórd:
you surróund him with fávour as with a shíeld.

Ant. It is you whom I invoke, O Lord. In the morning you hear me.

SCRIPTURE READING 2 Thess 3:10b–13

We gave you a rule when we were with you: not to let anyone have any food if he refused to do any work. Now we hear that there are some of you who are living in idleness, doing no work themselves but interfering with everyone else's. In the Lord Jesus Christ, we order and call on people of this kind to go on quietly working and earning the food that they eat. My brothers, never grow tired of doing what is right.

SHORT RESPONSORY
℟ Blessed be the Lord from age to age.
℣ He alone has wrought marvellous works.

WEEK I: MONDAY

INTERCESSIONS

As the new day begins let us praise Christ, in whom is the fulness of grace and the Spirit of God. ℟ Lord, give us your Spirit.

We praise you, Lord, – and we thank you for all your blessings. ℟

Give us peace of mind and generosity of heart; – grant us health and strength to do your will. ℟

May your love be with us during the day; – guide us in our work. ℟

Be with all those who have asked our prayers, – and grant them all their needs. ℟

Our Father

EVENING PRAYER

PSALMODY

Ant. Blessed are the pure in heart; they shall see God.

**Who shall be worthy to stand
before the Lord?** Psalm 14 (15)

You have come to Mount Sion to the city of the living God
(Heb 12:22)

> Lord, whó shall be admítted to your ténth
> and dwéll on your hóly móuntain?
>
> Hé who wálks without fáult;
> hé who ácts with jústice
> and spéaks the trúth from his héart;
> hé who does not slánder with his tóngue;
>
> hé who does no wróng to his bróther,
> who cásts no slúr on his néighbour,
> who hólds the gódless in disdáin,
> but hónours those who féar the Lórd;

hé who keeps his plédge, come what máy;
who tákes no ínterest on a lóan
and áccepts no bríbes against the ínnocent.
Such a mán will stand fírm for éver.

Ant. Blessed are the pure in heart: they shall see God.
Ant 2: God chose us in his Son and made us his adopted sons.

God, the Saviour   Canticle: Eph 1:3–10

Blessed be the God and Father
of our Lord Jesus Christ,
who has blessed us in Christ
with every spiritual blessing in the heavenly places.

He chose us in him
before the foundation of the world,
that we should be holy
and blameless before him.

He destined us in love
to be his sons through Jesus Christ,
according to the purpose of his will,
to the praise of his glorious grace
which he freely bestowed on us in the Beloved.

In him we have redemption through his blood,
the forgiveness of our trespasses,
according to the riches of his grace
which he lavished upon us.

He has made known to us
in all wisdom and insight
the mystery of his will,
according to his purpose
which he set forth in Christ.

WEEK I: MONDAY

> His purpose he set forth in Christ,
> as a plan for the fulness of time,
> to unite all things in him,
> things in heaven and things on earth.

Ant. God chose us in his Son and made us his adopted sons.

SCRIPTURE READING   Col 1:9b–11

We ask God to fill you with the knowledge of his will, with all the wisdom and understanding that his Spirit gives. Then you will be able to live as the Lord wants, and always do what pleases him. Your lives will be fruitful in all kinds of good works, and you will grow in your knowledge of God. May you be made strong with all the strength which comes from his glorious might, so that you may be able to endure everything with patience.

SHORT RESPONSORY

℟ Heal my soul for I have sinned against you.
℣ I said: 'Lord, have mercy on me.'

INTERCESSIONS

God our Father has bound himself to us in an everlasting covenant. In thankfulness and faith, we pray to him. ℟ Lord, bless your people!

In Christ you have given a new covenant to men: – may they know the greatness which they have inherited. ℟

Gather into one all who bear the name of Christian, – that the world may believe in the Christ you have sent. ℟

Pour out your love on our friends, and on all whom we know; – may they carry with them the gentleness of Christ. ℟

Comfort the dying; – may they know your saving love. ℟

Show your mercy to the dead; – may they find their rest in Christ. ℟

Our Father

Week I: Tuesday

MORNING PRAYER

PSALMODY
Ant. Praise is fitting for loyal hearts.

Praise of the providence of the Lord   Psalm 32 (33)

All things were made through him (Jn 1:3)

Ring out your jóy to the Lórd, O you júst;
for praise is fítting for lóyal héarts.

Give thánks to the Lórd upon the lýre
with a tén-stringed hárp sing him sóngs.
O síng him a sóng that is néw,
play lóudly, with áll your skíll.

For the wórd of the Lórd is fáithful
and áll his wórks to be trústed.
The Lórd loves jústice and ríght
and fílls the éarth with his lóve.

By his wórd the héavens were máde,
by the bréath of his móuth all the stárs.
He collécts the wáves of the ócean;
he stóres up the dépths of the séa.

Let all the éarth féar the Lórd,
all who líve in the wórld revére him.
He spóke; and it cáme to bé.
He commánded; it spráng into béing.

He frustrátes the desígns of the nátions,
he deféats the pláns of the péoples.
His ówn desígns shall stánd for éver,
the pláns of his héart from age to áge.

They are háppy, whose Gód is the Lórd,
the péople he has chósen as his ówn.
From the héavens the Lórd looks fórth,
he sées all the chíldren of mén.

From the pláce where he dwélls he gázes
on áll the dwéllers on the éarth,
he who shápes the héarts of them áll
and consíders áll their déeds.

A kíng is not sáved by his ármy,
nor a wárrior presérved by his stréngth.
A váin hope for sáfety is the hórse;
despíte its pówer it cannot sáve.

The Lórd looks on thóse who revére him,
on thóse who hópe in his lóve,
to réscue their sóuls from déath,
to kéep them alíve in fámine.

Our sóul is wáiting for the Lórd.
The Lórd is our hélp and our shíeld.
In hím do our héarts find jóy.
We trúst in his hóly náme.

May your lóve be upón us, O Lórd,
as we pláce all our hópe in yóu.

Ant. Praise is fitting for loyal hearts.

WEEK I: TUESDAY

SCRIPTURE READING Rom 13:11b, 12–13a

You know what hour it is, how it is full time now for you to wake from sleep. The night is far gone, the day is at hand. Let us then cast off the works of darkness and put on the armour of light; let us conduct ourselves becomingly as in the day.

SHORT RESPONSORY

℟ My helper is my God; I will place my trust in him.
℣ He is my refuge; he sets me free.

INTERCESSIONS

As Christians called to share the life of God, let us praise the Lord Jesus, the high priest of our faith. ℟ You are our Saviour and our God.
Almighty King; you have baptized us, and made us a royal priesthood; – may we offer you a constant sacrifice of praise. ℟
Help us to keep your commandments; – so that through your Holy Spirit we may dwell in you, and you in us. ℟
Everlasting Wisdom, come to us; – dwell with us and work in us today. ℟
Help us to be considerate and kind; – grant that we may bring joy, not pain, to those we meet. ℟
Our Father

EVENING PRAYER

PSALMODY

Ant. 1: The Lord will give victory to his anointed one.

Prayer for a king before battle Psalm 19 (20)

Whoever calls upon the name of the Lord will be saved (Acts 2:21)

May the Lórd ánswer in tíme of tríal;
may the náme of Jacob's Gód protéct you.

WEEK I: TUESDAY

> May he sénd you hélp from his shríne
> and gíve you suppórt from Síon.
> May he remémber áll your ófferings
> and réceive your sácrifice with fávour.
>
> May he gíve you your héart's desire
> and fulfíl every óne of your pláns.
> May we ríng out our jóy at your víctory
> and rejóice in the náme of our Gód.
> May the Lórd gránt all your práyers.
>
> I am súre now that the Lord
> will give víctory tó his anóinted,
> will replý from his hóly héaven
> with the mighty víctory of his hánd.
>
> Sóme trust in cháriots or hórses,
> but wé in the náme of the Lórd.
> Théy will collápse and fáll,
> but wé shall hóld and stand fírm.
>
> Give víctory to the kíng, O Lórd,
> give ánswer on the dáy we cáll.

Ant. The Lord will give victory to his anointed one.
Ant. 2: Lord, you made us a kingdom and priests to serve our God.

Hymn of the redeemed   Canticle: Rev 4:11; 5: 9, 10, 12

> Worthy are you, our Lord and God,
> to receive glory and honour and power,
> for you created all things,
> and by your will they existed and were created.
>
> Worthy are you, O Lord,
> to take the scroll and to open its seals,
> for you were slain,

WEEK I: TUESDAY

and by your blood you ransomed men for God
from every tribe and tongue and people and nation.

You have made us a kingdom and priests to our God,
and we shall reign on earth.

Worthy is the Lamb who was slain,
to receive power and wealth,
and wisdom and might,
and honour and glory and blessing.

Ant. Lord, you made us a kingdom and priests to serve our God.

SCRIPTURE READING   1 Jn 3:1a, 2
Think of the love that the Father has lavished on us,
by letting us be called God's children;
and that is what we are.
My dear people, we are already the children of God
but what we are to be in the future has not yet been
    revealed;
we shall be like him
because we shall see him as he really is.

SHORT RESPONSORY
- ℟ Your word, O Lord, will endure for ever.
- ℣ Your truth will last from age to age.

INTERCESSIONS
Through Christ we are sons of God: in him we see what we shall be when we come to the Father. With confidence we pray: ℟
Lord, in your mercy, hear our prayer.
Guide leaders and governments: – give them wisdom and integrity. ℟
You are the Lord and source of our freedom: – bring those in captivity of mind or body to the freedom of the children of God. ℟

WEEK I: TUESDAY

Give courage and strength to the young. – Help them to choose their work, and make the right decisions for their way of life. ℟

Give patient tolerance to all who are no longer young; – open the hearts of the young to accept from them understanding and love. ℟

Receive the departed into your eternal kingdom; – sustain our hope to reign with you for ever. ℟

Our Father

Week 1: Wednesday

MORNING PRAYER

PSALMODY
Ant. In your light, God, we see light.

**The evil of the sinner;
the goodness of the Lord** Psalm 35 (36)

The man who follows me will not walk in darkness, but he will have the light of life for his guide (Jn 8:12)

Sín spéaks to the sínner
in the dépths of his héart.
There ís no féar of Gód
befóre his éyes.

He so flátters himsélf in his mínd
that he knóws not his guílt.
In his móuth are míschief and decéit.
All wísdom is góne.

He plóts the deféat of góodness
as he líes on his béd.
He has sét his fóot on evil wáys,
he clíngs to what is évil.

Your lóve, Lord, réaches to héaven;
your trúth to the skies.
Your jústice is líke God's móuntain,
your júdgments like the déep.

WEEK I: WEDNESDAY

>To both mán and béast you give protéction.
>O Lórd, how précious is your lóve.
>My Gód, the sóns of mén
>find réfuge in the shélter of your wíngs.
>
>They féast on the riches of your hóuse;
>they drínk from the stréam of your delíght.
>In yóu is the sóurce of lífe
>and ín your light we see líght.
>
>Keep on lóving thóse who knów you,
>doing jústice for úpright héarts.
>Let the fóot of the próud not crúsh me
>nor the hánd of the wícked cast me óut.
>
>Sée how the évil-doers fáll!
>Flung dówn, they shall néver aríse.

Ant. In your light, God, we see light.

SCRIPTURE READING Tob 4:16–17, 19–20
Do to no one what you would not want done to you. Give your bread to those who are hungry, and your clothes to those who are naked. Ask advice of every wise person. Bless the Lord God in everything; beg him to guide your ways and bring your paths and purposes to their end.

SHORT RESPONSORY
℟ Bend my heart to your will, O God.
℣ By your word, give me life.

INTERCESSIONS
We give thanks to Christ and we praise him because he was not ashamed to call us his brothers. ℟ Lord Jesus, we are your brothers.

WEEK I: WEDNESDAY

Help us to live the new life of Easter, – so that men may know through us the power of your love. ℟

Every day is a proof of your love: – As you bring us to this new day, make us new in mind and in heart. ℟

Teach us to see you present in all men; – help us to recognize you most of all in those who suffer. ℟

May our lives today be filled with your compassion; – give us the spirit of forgiveness and a generous heart. ℟

Our Father

EVENING PRAYER

PSALMODY
Ant. 1: The Lord is my light and my help; whom shall I fear?

Trust in time of affliction   Psalm 26 (27)

Behold, the place where God dwells among men (Rev 21:3)

> The Lórd is my líght and my hélp;
> whóm shall I féar?
> The Lórd is the strónghold of my life;
> before whóm shall I shrínk?
>
> When évil-dóers draw néar
> to devóur my flésh,
> it is théy, my énemies and fóes,
> who stúmble and fáll.
>
> Though an ármy encámp agáinst me
> my héart would not féar.
> Though wár break óut agáinst me
> even thén would I trúst.
>
> There is óne thing I ásk of the Lórd,
> for thís I lóng,

WEEK I: WEDNESDAY

to líve in the hóuse of the Lórd,
all the dáys of my life,
to sávour the swéetness of the Lórd,
to behóld his témple.

For thére he keeps me sáfe in his tént
in the dáy of évil.
He hídes me in the shélter of his tént,
on a róck he sets me sáfe.

And nów my héad shall be ráised
above my fóes who surróund me
and I shall óffer withín his tént
a sácrifice of jóy.

I will síng and make músic for the Lórd.

O Lórd, hear my vóice when I cáll;
have mércy and ánswer.
Of yóu my héart has spóken:
'Seek his fáce.'

It is your fáce, O Lórd, that I séek;
híde not your fáce.
Dismíss not your sérvant in ánger;
yóu have been my hélp.

Dó not abándon or forsáke me,
O Gód my hélp!
Though fáther and móther forsáke me,
The Lórd will recéive me.

Instrúct me, Lórd, in your wáy;
on an éven path léad me.
When they líe in ámbush protéct me
from my énemy's gréed.
False wítnesses ríse agáinst me,
bréathing out fúry.

I am súre I shall sée the Lord's góodness
in the lánd of the líving.
Hope in hím, hold fírm and take héart.
Hópe in the Lórd!

Ant. 1: The Lord is my light and my help; whom shall I fear?

SCRIPTURE READING   Jas 1:22, 25
You must do what the word tells you, and not just listen to it and deceive yourselves. But the man who looks steadily at the perfect law of freedom and makes that his habit – not listening and then forgetting, but actively putting it into practice – will be happy in all that he does.

SHORT RESPONSORY
℟ Redeem me, Lord, and show me your mercy.
℣ Do not cast me away with sinners.

INTERCESSIONS
The world is ablaze with the glory of God, who cares for his chosen people with infinite love. In the name of the Church we pray: ℟ Lord, show your love to all men.
Be mindful of your Church: – keep her free from evil and make her perfect in your love. ℟
Let all peoples acknowledge that you alone are God, and that Jesus Christ is your Son; – give them the light of faith. ℟
Grant to those around us all that they need, – so that they may know thankfulness and live in peace. ℟
Keep us mindful of those whose work is hard and unrewarding: – may we give every man the respect which is his right. ℟
Give peace to those who have died today; – grant them eternal rest. ℟
Our Father

Week 1: Thursday

MORNING PRAYER

PSALMODY
Ant. Awake, lyre and harp, I will awake the dawn.

Morning prayer in time of affliction   Psalm 56 (57)

This psalm celebrates the passion of Christ (St Augustine)

Have mércy on me, Gód, have mércy
for in yóu my sóul has taken réfuge.
In the shádow of your wíngs I take réfuge
till the stórms of destrúction pass bý.

I cáll to Gód the Most Hígh,
to Gód who has álways been my hélp.
May he sénd from héaven and sáve me
and sháme thóse who assáil me.

May Gód send his trúth and his lóve.

My sóul lies dówn among líons,
who would devóur the sóns of mén.
Their téeth are spéars and árrows,
their tóngue a shárpened swórd.

O Gód, aríse above the héavens;
may your glóry shine on éarth!

They láid a snáre for my stéps,
my sóul was bowed dówn.
They dúg a pít in my páth
but féll in it themsélves.

WEEK I: THURSDAY

My héart is réady, O Gód,
my héart is réady.
I will síng, I will síng your práise.
Awáke my sóul,
awáke lýre and hárp,
I will awáke the dáwn.

I will thánk you Lórd among the péoples,
among the nátions I will práise you
for your lóve réaches to the héavens
and your trúth to the skíes.

O Gód, aríse above the héavens;
may your glory shine on earth!

Ant. Awake, lyre and harp, I will awake the dawn.

SCRIPTURE READING Is 66:1–2
Thus says the Lord:
With heaven my throne
and earth my footstool,
what house could you build me,
what place could you make for my rest?
All of this was made by my hand
and all of this is mine – it is the Lord who speaks.
But my eyes are drawn to the man
of humbled and contrite spirit,
who trembles at my word.

SHORT RESPONSORY
℟ I called with all my heart; Lord, hear me.
℣ I will keep your commandments.

WEEK I: THURSDAY

INTERCESSIONS

Let us begin this new day with Christ, thanking him for all he has brought to us, and asking him to bless us. R/ Lord, accept and bless our work today.

You offered yourself to the Father on our behalf: – join our offering with yours. R/

You are gentle and humble of heart: – teach us to receive others as you did. R/

As each day begins, may your light rise in our hearts; – may it shine forth in charity to the world. R/

Show your mercy to those who are sick: – may each new day increase their trust in you. R/

Our Father

EVENING PRAYER

PSALMODY

Ant. Happy the man to whom the Lord imputes no guilt.

Happy is the man whose offence is forgiven　　Psalm 31 (32)

David says that a man is blessed if God considers him righteous, irrespective of good deeds (Rom 4:6)

Happy the mán whose offénce is forgíven,
whose sín is remítted.
O háppy the mán to whom the Lórd
impútes no guílt,
in whose spírit is no guíle.

I kept it sécret and my fráme was wásted.
I groáned all day lóng
for níght and dáy your hánd
was héavy upón me.
Indéed, my stréngth was dried úp
as by the súmmer's héat.

But nów I have acknówledged my síns;
my guílt I did not híde.
I sáid: 'I will conféss
my offénce to the Lórd.'
And yóu, Lórd, have forgíven
the guílt of my sín.

So let évery good mán pray to yóu
in the tíme of néed.
The flóods of wáter may reach hígh
but hím they shall not réach.
Yóu are my híding place, O Lórd;
you sáve me from distréss.
You surróund me with crìes of delíverance.

I will instrúct you and téach you
the wáy you should gó;
I will gíve you cóunsel
with my éye upón you.

Be not like hórse and múle, unintélligent,
needing brídle and bít,
élse they wíll not appróach you.
Many sórrows has the wícked
but hé who trústs in the Lórd,
loving mércy surróunds him.

Rejóice, rejóice in the Lórd,
exúlt, you júst!
O cóme, ríng out your jóy,
all you úpright of héart.

Ant. Happy the man to whom the Lord imputes no guilt.

SCRIPTURE READING   1 Pet 1:6–9
This is a cause of great joy for you, even though you may for a short time have to bear being plagued by all sorts of trials; so

WEEK I: THURSDAY

that, when Jesus Christ is revealed, your faith will have been tested and proved like gold – only it is more precious than gold, which is corruptible even though it bears testing by fire – and then you will have praise and glory and honour. You did not see him, yet you love him; and still without seeing him, you are already filled with a joy so glorious that it cannot be described, because you believe; and you are sure of the end to which your faith looks forward, that is, the salvation of your souls.

SHORT RESPONSORY
℟ The Lord fed us with finest wheat.
℣ He filled us with honey from the rock.

INTERCESSIONS
Let us make our prayer to the God of our salvation because all our hope rests in him. ℟ Father, our trust is in you.

Father, you established a covenant with men: – we trust in you, for you are faithful to your word. ℟

Send workers into the harvest, – and bring the world to the knowledge and love of you. ℟

May the unity of the Church be formed by love and understanding; – gather us together through the gifts of your Holy Spirit. ℟

Help men to create a community where justice and peace may flourish: – be with us, lest we labour in vain. ℟

Be mindful of the dead, especially those we have known; – have mercy on those who have given us their help. ℟

Our Father

Week 1: Friday

MORNING PRAYER

PSALMODY
Ant. Lord, you will be pleased with lawful sacrifice offered on your altar.

Have mercy on me, God Psalm 50 (51)

You must be made new in mind and spirit, and put on the new nature of God's creating (Eph 4:23, 24)

Have mércy on me, Gód, in your kíndness.
In your compássion blot óut my offénce.
O wásh me more and móre from my guílt
and cléanse me fróm my sín.

My offénces trúly I knów them;
my sín is álways befóre me.
Against yóu, you alóne, have I sinned;
what is évil in your síght I have dóne.

That you may be jústified whén you give séntence
and be withóut repróach when you júdge,
O sée, in guílt I was born,
a sínner was I concéived.

Indéed you love trúth in the héart;
then in the sécret of my héart teach me wisdom.
O púrify me, thén I shall be cléan;
O wásh me, I shall be whíter than snów.

WEEK I: FRIDAY

Make me héar rejóicing and gládness,
that the bónes you have crúshed may revíve.
From my síns turn awáy your fáce
and blót out áll my guílt.

A púre heart créate for me, O Gód,
put a stéadfast spírit withín me.
Do not cást me awáy from your présence,
nor depríve me of your hóly spírit.

Give me agáin the jóy of your hélp;
with a spírit of férvour sustáin me,
that I may téach transgréssors your wáys
and sínners may retúrn to yóu.

O réscue me, Gód, my hélper,
and my tóngue shall ríng out your góodness.
O Lórd, ópen my líps
and my móuth shall decláre your práise.

For in sácrifice you táke no delíght,
burnt óffering from mé you would refúse,
my sácrifice, a cóntrite spírit.
A húmbled, contrite héart you will not spúrn.

In your góodness, show fávour to Síon:
rebuíld the wálls of Jerúsalem.
Thén you will be pléased with lawful sácrifice,
hólocausts óffered on your áltar.

Ant. Lord, you will be pleased with lawful sacrifice offered on your altar.

SCRIPTURE READING   Eph 4:29–32
Do not use harmful words in talking. Use only helpful words, the kind that build up and provide what is needed, so that what you say will do good to those who hear you. And do not make

WEEK I: FRIDAY

God's Holy Spirit sad; for the Spirit is God's mark of ownership on you, a guarantee that the Day will come when God will set you free. Get rid of all bitterness, passion, and anger. No more shouting or insults. No more hateful feelings of any sort. Instead, be kind and tender-hearted to one another, and forgive one another, as God has forgiven you in Christ.

SHORT RESPONSORY
℟ In the morning let me know your love.
℣ Make me know the way I should walk.

INTERCESSIONS
Lord Jesus Christ, we thank you. Through your cross and resurrection you offer freedom and hope to those ready to receive them. ℟ Lord, show us your loving-kindness.
We are children of the day: – help us to live in the light of your presence. ℟
Guide our thoughts, our words, our actions: – so that what we do today may be pleasing to you. ℟
Help us to avoid wrongdoing: – show us your mercy and love. ℟
Through your passion and death you have won life for us: – give us the strength of your Holy Spirit. ℟
Our Father

WEEK I: FRIDAY

EVENING PRAYER

PSALMODY
Ant. 1: The Lord of hosts is with us: the God of Jacob is our stronghold.

God is our refuge and strength   Psalm 45 (46)

They will call his name 'Immanuel' which means 'God with us' (Mt 1:23)

God is for us a réfuge and stréngth,
a hélper close at hánd, in tíme of distréss:
so wé shall nót féar though the éarth should róck,
though the móuntains fáll into the dépths of the séa,
even thóugh its wáters ráge and fóam,
even thóugh the móuntains be sháken by its wáves.

The Lórd of hósts is wíth us:
the Gód of Jácob is our strónghold.

The wáters of a ríver give jóy to God's cíty,
the hóly pláce where the Móst High dwélls.
God is withín, it cánnot be sháken;
God will hélp it at the dáwning of the dáy.
Nátions are in túmult, kíngdoms are sháken;
he lífts his vóice, the éarth shrinks awáy.

The Lórd of hósts is wíth us:
the Gód of Jácob is our strónghold.

Cóme, consíder the wórks of the Lórd
the redóubtable déeds he has dóne on the éarth.
He puts an énd to wárs over áll the éarth;
the bów he bréaks, the spéar he snáps.
He búrns the shíelds with fíre.
'Be stíll and knów that I am Gód,
supréme among the nátions, supréme on the éarth!'

WEEK I: FRIDAY

The Lórd of hósts is wíth us:
the Gód of Jácob is our strónghold.

Ant. The Lord of hosts is with us: the God of Jacob is our stronghold.
Ant. 2: All the peoples will come and adore you, Lord.

Hymn of Adoration
Canticle: Rev 15:3-4

Great and wonderful are your deeds,
O Lord God the Almighty!
Just and true are your ways,
O King of the ages!

Who shall not fear and glorify your name, O Lord?
For you alone are holy.
All nations shall come and worship you,
for your judgments have been revealed.

Ant. All the peoples will come and adore you, Lord.

SCRIPTURE READING Rom 15:1-3
We who are strong ought to bear with the failings of the weak, and not to please ourselves; let each of us please his neighbour for his good, to edify him. For Christ did not please himself; but, as it is written, The reproaches of those who reproached you fell on me.

SHORT RESPONSORY
℟ Christ loved us and has washed away our sins with his blood.
℣ He made us a line of kings, priests to serve God.

INTERCESSIONS
God is our loving Father, who cares for us and knows all our needs. With confidence we pray: ℟ Father, may we find rest in your love.

WEEK I: FRIDAY

Christ, your Son, suffered and died for the Church: – be with all Christians who are suffering tonight. ℟

Bring to the sick your comfort and healing; – strengthen them through the victory of Calvary. ℟

Be near to us, almighty Father, – for you alone can save us from the evils that threaten us. ℟

Strengthen us in the hour of death: – let us know your peace. ℟

Bring the dead into your light: – comfort them with your presence. ℟

Our Father

Week 1: Saturday

MORNING PRAYER

PSALMODY
Ant. My eyes watch for you before dawn.

Psalm 118 (119): 145–152 XIX (Koph)

I cáll with my héart; Lord, héar me,
I will kéep your commánds.
I cáll upón you, sáve me
and I will do your wíll.

I ríse before dáwn and cry for hélp,
I hópe in your wórd.
My éyes wátch through the níght
to pónder your prómise.

In your lóve hear my vóice, O Lórd;
give me lífe by your decrées.
Those who hárm me unjústly draw néar:
they are fár from your láw.

But you, O Lórd, are clóse:
your commánds are trúth.
Lóng have I knówn that your wíll
is estáblished for éver.

Ant. My eyes watch for you before dawn.
Ant. 2: O praise the Lord, all you nations.

WEEK I: SATURDAY

Praise to the God of mercy　　　　　　　　Psalm 116(117)

I ask the nations to give praise to God for his mercy
(Rom 15:8–9)

> O práise the Lórd, all you nátions,
> accláim him all you péoples!
>
> Stróng is his lóve for ús;
> he is fáithful for éver.

Ant. O praise the Lord, all you nations.

SCRIPTURE READING　　　　　　　　　　　　2 Pet 1:10–11
Brothers, you have been called and chosen: work all the harder to justify it by good deeds. If you do all these things there is no danger that you will ever fall away. In this way you will be granted admittance into the eternal kingdom of our Lord and saviour Jesus Christ.

SHORT RESPONSORY
℟ I called to you, Lord, you are my refuge.
℣ You are all I have in the land of the living.

INTERCESSIONS
Christ became man to make us sons of God and he intercedes for us before God our Father. Let us thank him for his loving mercy, and pray: ℟ Open to us the treasures of your love.
You have enlightened us in baptism: – we consecrate our day to you. ℟
Fill us with praise of you today: – may we take your word with us wherever we may go. ℟
Teach us to respond to your word like Mary our Mother: – may your word be fruitful in us. ℟

Give us courage when things go wrong: – strengthen us with faith in you, with hope in your promises and with love of your will. ℟
Our Father

EVENING PRAYER

PSALMODY
Ant. 1: Your word is a lamp for my steps, Lord, alleluia.

Meditation on the word of God in the Law
Psalm 118 (119): 105–112 XIV (Nun)

This is my commandment; that you love each other (Jn 15:12)

Your wórd is a lámp for my stéps
and a líght for my páth.
I have swórn and have máde up my mínd
to obéy your decrées.

Lórd, I am déeply afflícted:
by your wórd give me lífe.
Accépt, Lord, the hómage of my líps
and téach me your decrées.

Though I cárry my life in my hánds,
I remémber your láw.
Though the wícked trý to ensnáre me
I do not stráy from your précepts.

Your wíll is my héritage for éver,
the jóy of my héart.
I sét myself to cárry out your wíll
in fúlness, for éver.

Ant. Your word is a lamp for my steps, Lord, alleluia.

WEEK I: SATURDAY

Ant. 2: Let every creature, in heaven and on earth, bend the knee at the name of Jesus, alleluia.

Christ, the servant of God   Canticle: Phil 2:6–11

Though he was in the form of God,
Jesus did not count equality with God a thing to be grasped.

He emptied himself,
taking the form of a servant,
being born in the likeness of men.

And being found in human form,
he humbled himself and became obedient unto death,
even death on a cross.

Therefore God has highly exalted him
and bestowed on him the name which is above every name,

That at the name of Jesus every knee should bow,
in heaven and on earth and under the earth,

And every tongue confess that Jesus Christ is Lord,
to the glory of God the Father.

Ant. Let every creature, in heaven and on earth, bend the knee at the name of Jesus, alleluia.

SCRIPTURE READING   Col 1:3–6a
May God our Father and the Lord Jesus Christ give you grace and peace. We always give thanks to God, the Father of our Lord Jesus Christ, when we pray for you. For we have heard of your faith in Christ Jesus, and of your love for all God's people. When the true message, the Good News, first came to you, you heard of the hope it offers. So your faith and love are based on what you hope for, which is kept safe for you in heaven. The gospel is bringing blessings and spreading through the whole world, just as it has among you.

WEEK I: SATURDAY

SHORT RESPONSORY

℟ From the rising of the sun to its setting, great is the name of the Lord.

℣ High above the heavens is his glory.

INTERCESSIONS

God our Father leads us forward with great love towards the joyful day when we enter his rest. ℟ Our hope is all in you, Lord God.

Father, we pray for N., our Pope, and N., our bishop: – guide them and bless them in their work. ℟

Help the sick to share their sufferings with Christ: – may they know in him the fulness of life and love. ℟

Lord, you found nowhere to lay your head: – make us aware of the needs of the homeless today. ℟

Bless those who work on the land: – may we receive the fruits of the earth with thankfulness. ℟

Father, have mercy on those who have died in the peace of Christ: – receive them into the home you have prepared for them. ℟

Our Father

Week 2: Sunday

MORNING PRAYER

PSALMODY
Ant. 1: Let us sing a hymn to our God, alleluia.

Let every creature praise the Lord Canticle: Dan 3:52–57

The Creator is blessed for ever (Rom 1:25)

You are blest, Lord God of our fathers.
To you glory and praise for evermore.

Blest your glorious holy name.
To you glory and praise for evermore.

You are blest in the temple of your glory.
To you glory and praise for evermore.

You are blest who gaze into the depths.
To you glory and praise for evermore.

You are blest in the firmament of heaven.
To you glory and praise for evermore.

You who walk on the wings of the wind:
To you glory and praise for evermore.

May they bless you, the saints and the angels.
To you glory and praise for evermore.

From the heavens, the earth and the sea,
To you glory and praise for evermore.

WEEK 2: SUNDAY

You are blest, Lord God of our fathers.
To you glory and praise for evermore.

Ant. Let us sing a hymn to our God, alleluia.
Ant. 2: Praise the Lord for his surpassing greatness, alleluia.

Praise the Lord Psalm 150

Sing praise in your spirit, sing praise with your soul, that is: give glory to God in both your soul and your body (Hesychius).

Práise Gód in his hóly pláce,
práise him in his míghty héavens.
Práise him for his pówerful déeds,
práise his surpássing gréatness.

O práise him with sóund of trúmpet,
práise him with lúte and hárp.
Práise him with tímbrel and dánce,
práise him with strings and pípes.

O práise him with resóunding cýmbals,
práise him with cláshing of cýmbals.
Let éverything that líves and that bréathes
give práise to the Lórd.

Ant. Praise the Lord for his surpassing greatness, alleluia.

SCRIPTURE READING Ezek 36:25–27
I shall pour clean water over you and you will be cleansed; I shall cleanse you of all your defilement and all your idols. I shall give you a new heart, and put a new spirit in you; I shall remove the heart of stone from your bodies and give you a heart of flesh instead. I shall put my spirit in you, and make you keep my laws and sincerely respect my observances.

WEEK 2: SUNDAY

SHORT RESPONSORY
℟ We give thanks to you, O God, and call upon your name.
Repeat ℟
℣ We recount your wonderful deeds.

INTERCESSIONS
Let us thank our Saviour, who came into this world that God might be with us. ℟ We praise you, O Lord, and we thank you.
We welcome you with praise, you are the Daystar, the first fruits from the dead: – let us rise with you to walk in the light of Easter. ℟
Help us on this day of rest to see goodness in all your creatures: – open our eyes and our hearts to your love in the world. ℟
Lord, we meet around your table as your family: – help us to see that our bitterness is forgotten, our discord is resolved, and our sins are forgiven. ℟
We pray for all Christian families: – may your Spirit deepen their unity in faith and love. ℟
Our Father

EVENING PRAYER

PSALMODY
Ant. 1: The man with clean hands and pure heart will climb the mountain of the Lord.

The Lord comes to his temple Psalm 23 (24)

The gates of heaven were opened to Christ because he was lifted up in the flesh (St Irenaeus)

> The Lórd's is the éarth and its fúlness,
> the wórld and áll its péoples.
> It is hé who sét it on the séas;
> on the wáters he máde it fírm.

WEEK 2: SUNDAY

Who shall clímb the móuntain of the Lórd?
Who shall stánd in his hóly pláce?
The mán with clean hánds and pure héart,
who desíres not wórthless thíngs,
who has not swórn so as to decéive his néighbour.

He shall recéive bléssings from the Lórd
and rewárd from the Gód who sáves him.
Súch are the mén who séek him,
seek the fáce of the Gód of Jácob.

O gátes, lift hígh your héads;
grow hígher, áncient dóors.
Let him énter, the kíng of glóry!

Whó is the kíng of glóry?
The Lórd, the míghty, the váliant,
the Lórd, the váliant in wár.

O gátes, lift hígh your héads;
grow hígher, áncient dóors,
Let him énter, the kíng of glóry!

Who is hé, the kíng of glóry?
Hé, the Lórd of ármies,
hé is the kíng of glóry.

Ant. The man with clean hands and pure heart will climb the mountain of the Lord.
Ant. 2: The Lord has satisfied and filled with good things those who hungered for justice.

The Canticle of Mary

Lk 1:46–55

My soul rejoices in the Lord

My soul glorifies the Lord,
my spirit rejoices in God, my Saviour.

WEEK 2: SUNDAY

He looks on his servant in her lowliness;
henceforth all ages will call me blessed.

The Almighty works marvels for me.
Holy his name!
His mercy is from age to age,
on those who fear him.

He puts forth his arm in strength
and scatters the proud-hearted.
He casts the mighty from their thrones
and raises the lowly.

He fills the starving with good things,
sends the rich away empty.

He protects Israel, his servant,
remembering his mercy,
the mercy promised to our fathers,
to Abraham and his sons for ever.

Ant. The Lord has satisfied and filled with good things those who hungered for justice.

SCRIPTURE READING 2 Thess 2:13–14
We feel that we must be continually thanking God for you, brothers whom the Lord loves, because God chose you as first fruits to be saved by the sanctifying Spirit and by faith in the truth. Through the Good News that we brought he called you to this so that you should share the glory of our Lord Jesus Christ.

SHORT RESPONSORY
R/ Great is our Lord; great is his might.
V His wisdom can never be measured.

WEEK 2: SUNDAY

INTERCESSIONS

Through the gospel, the Lord Jesus calls us to share in his glory. Let us make our prayer with him to our heavenly Father. ℟
Lord, in your mercy hear our prayer.

We pray for all nations: – that they may seek the way that leads to peace, that human rights and freedom may be everywhere respected, and that the world's resources may be generously shared. ℟

We pray for the Church: – that her leaders may be faithful ministers of your word, and that all her members may be strong in faith and hope and that you may be recognized in the love she bears to all. ℟

We pray for our families, and the community in which we live: – that we may find you in them. ℟

We pray for ourselves: – that in the coming week we may serve others in our work, and find peace when we rest. ℟

We pray for the faithful departed: – that through your mercy they may rest in peace. ℟

Our Father

Week 2: Monday

MORNING PRAYER

PSALMODY
Ant. 1: When can I enter and see the face of God?

The exile's nostalgia for the Lord's temple   Psalm 41 (42)

Let all who are thirsty come; all who want it may have the water of life (Rev 22:17)

Líke the déer that yéarns
for rúnning stréams,
só my sóul is yéarning
for yóu, my Gód.

My sóul is thírsting for Gód,
the Gód of my lífe;
whén can I énter and sée
the fáce of Gód?

My téars have becóme my bréad,
by níght, by dáy,
as I héar it sáid all the day lóng:
'Whére is your Gód?'

Thése things will Í remémber
as I póur out my sóul:
how I would léad the rejóicing crówd
into the hóuse of Gód,
amid crées of gládness and thanksgíving,
the thróng wild with jóy.

Whý are you cast dówn, my sóul,
why gróan withín me?
Hope in Gód; I will práise him stíll,
my sáviour and my Gód.

My sóul is cast dówn withín me
and I thínk of yóu,
from the cóuntry of Jórdan and Mount Hérmon,
from the Híll of Mízar.

Déep is cálling on déep,
in the róar of wáters:
your tórrents and áll your wáves
swept óver mé.

By dáy the Lórd will sénd
his lóving kíndness;
by níght I will síng to hím,
praise the Gód of my lífe.

I will sáy to Gód, my róck:
'Whý have you forgótten me?
Whý do Í go móurning
oppréssed by the fóe?'

With críes that píerce me to the héart,
my énemies revíle me,
sáying to me áll the day lóng:
'Whére is your Gód?'

Whý are you cast dówn, my sóul,
why gróan withín me?
Hope in Gód; I will práise him stíll,
my sáviour and my Gód.

Ant. When can I enter and see the face of God?

WEEK 2: MONDAY

SCRIPTURE READING   Jer 15:16

When your words came, I devoured them:
your word was my delight
and the joy of my heart;
for I was called by your name,
Lord, God of Sabaoth.

SHORT RESPONSORY

℟ Rejoice in the Lord, O you just; for praise is fitting for loyal hearts. Repeat ℟
℣ Sing to him a new song.

INTERCESSIONS

Christ has given us all a share in his priesthood. We offer our prayers and ourselves in union with him. ℟ Lord, accept our love and service.
Jesus Christ, you are the eternal priest: – make this morning's offering acceptable to the Father. ℟
Lord, you are love itself: – grant that we may love you. ℟
Give us today the fruits of the Holy Spirit: – make us patient, kind and gentle. ℟
Give us the discernment to know the needs of our neighbours, – and give us the courage to love them as brothers. ℟
Our Father

WEEK 2: MONDAY

EVENING PRAYER

PSALMODY
Ant. 1: Those who seek the Lord lack no blessing.

The Lord is the salvation of the just Psalm 33 (34)

You have tasted and seen that the Lord is sweet (1 Pet 2:3)

I

I will bléss the Lórd at all tímes,
his práise álways on my líps;
in the Lórd my sóul shall make its bóast.
The húmble shall héar and be glád.

Glórify the Lórd with mé.
Togéther let us práise his náme.
I sóught the Lórd and he ánswered me;
from all my térrors he sét me frée.

Lóok towards hím and be rádiant;
let your fáces nót be abáshed.
This póor man cálled; the Lord héard him
and réscued him from áll his distréss.

The ángel of the Lórd is encámped
around thóse who revére him, to réscue them.
Taste and sée that the Lórd is góod.
He is háppy who seeks réfuge in hím.

Revére the Lórd, you his sáints.
They lack nóthing, thóse who revére him.
Strong líons suffer wánt and go húngry
but thóse who seek the Lórd lack no bléssing.

Ant. Those who seek the Lord lack no blessing.
Ant. 2: Let peace be all your quest and aim.

WEEK 2: MONDAY

II
Cóme, chíldren, and héar me
that I may téach you the féar of the Lórd.
Who is hé who lóngs for lífe
and many dáys, to enjóy his prospérity?

Then kéep your tóngue from évil
and your líps from spéaking decéit.
Turn asíde from évil and do góod;
séek and stríve after péace.

The Lórd turns his fáce against the wícked
to destróy their remémbrance from the éarth.
The Lórd turns his éyes to the júst
and his éars to théir appéal.

They cáll and the Lórd héars
and réscues them in áll their distréss.
The Lord is clóse to the bróken-héarted;
those whose spírit is crúshed he will sáve.

Mány are the tríals of the júst man
but from them áll the Lórd will réscue him.
He will keep guárd over áll his bónes,
not óne of his bónes shall be bróken.

Évil brings déath to the wícked;
those who háte the góod are dóomed.
The Lord ránsoms the sóuls of his sérvants.
Those who híde in him shall nót be condémned.

Ant. Let peace be all your quest and aim.

SCRIPTURE READING   1 Thess 2:13
Another reason why we constantly thank God for you is that as soon as you heard the message we brought you as God's message, you accepted it for what it really is, God's message and

WEEK 2: MONDAY

not some human thinking; and it is still a living power among you who believe it.

SHORT RESPONSORY

℟ Let my prayer come before you, O Lord.
℣ Let it rise in your presence like incense.

INTERCESSIONS

Let us give thanks to Christ our Lord who loves and cherishes his Church. ℟ Be near us, Lord, this evening.

Lord Jesus grant that all men may be saved, – and come to knowledge of the truth. ℟

Protect Pope N. and N., our Bishop: – help them, Lord, in your strength and mercy. ℟

Support those who meet with difficulty and disappointment: – renew their confidence and sense of purpose. ℟

Christ our loving Lord, in your kindness be with the sick and the poor, the weak and the dying: – bring them your comfort. ℟

We commend to you all those who, in their lifetime, shared in the sacred ministry: – let them praise you for ever in heaven. ℟

Our Father

Week 2: Tuesday

MORNING PRAYER

PSALMODY
Ant. 1: Lord, send forth your light and your truth.

Desire for God's temple
Psalm 42 (43)

I, the light, have come into the world (Jn 12:46)

> Defénd me, O Gód, and plead my cáuse
> against a gódless nátion.
> From decéitful and cúnning mén
> réscue me, O Gód.
>
> Since yóu, O Gód, are my strónghold,
> whý have you rejécted me?
> Why do Í go móurning
> oppréssed by the fóe?
>
> O sénd forth your líght and your trúth;
> let thése be my guíde.
> Let them bríng me to your hóly móuntain
> to the pláce where you dwéll.
>
> And I will cóme to the áltar of Gód,
> the Gód of my jóy.
> My redéemer, I will thánk you on the hárp,
> O Gód, my Gód.

Whý are you cast dówn, my sóul,
why gróan withín me?
Hope in Gód; I will práise him stíll,
my sáviour and my Gód.

Ant. Lord, send forth your light and your truth.
Ant. 2: Let us serve the Lord in holiness, and he will deliver us from the hands of our enemies.

The Canticle of Zechariah
Lk 1:68–79

The Messiah and the one who was sent before him

Blessed be the Lord, the God of Israel!
He has visited his people and redeemed them.

He has raised up for us a mighty saviour
in the house of David his servant,
as he promised by the lips of holy men,
those who were his prophets from of old.

A saviour who would free us from our foes,
from the hands of all who hate us.
So his love for our fathers is fulfilled
and his holy covenant remembered.

He swore to Abraham our father to grant us,
that free from fear, and saved from the hands of our foes,
we might serve him in holiness and justice
all the days of our life in his presence.

As for you, little child,
you shall be called a prophet of God, the Most High.
You shall go ahead of the Lord
to prepare his ways before him,

To make known to his people their salvation
through forgiveness of all their sins,

WEEK 2: TUESDAY

> the loving-kindness of the heart of our God
> who visits us like the dawn from on high.
>
> He will give light to those in darkness,
> those who dwell in the shadow of death,
> and guide us into the way of peace.

Ant. Let us serve the Lord in holiness, and he will deliver us from the hands of our enemies.

SCRIPTURE READING   1 Thess 5:4-5
It is not as if you live in the dark, my brothers, for that Day to overtake you like a thief. No, you are all sons of light and sons of the day: we do not belong to the night or to darkness.

SHORT RESPONSORY
℟ Hear my cry, Lord, for I hope in your word.
℣ I rise before dawn and call for help.

INTERCESSIONS
Let us bless our Saviour, who by his rising to new life has freed the world from fear. ℟ Lord, lead us to the truth.
Lord Jesus, as this day begins we remember that you are risen, – and therefore we look to the future with confidence. ℟
We offer you our prayer this morning, – take to yourself our cares, our hopes, and our needs. ℟
Deepen in us our love for you today, – so that in all things we may find our good, and the good of others. ℟
Lord Jesus, we pray that through our own troubles, we may learn to feel the sufferings of others: – help us to show them your compassion. ℟
Our Father

WEEK 2: TUESDAY

EVENING PRAYER

PSALMODY
Ant. 1: You cannot serve both God and wealth.

The uselessness of riches
Psalm 48 (49)

The rich man will find it very hard to enter the kingdom of heaven (Mt 19:23)

I
Héar this, áll you peoples,
give héed, all who dwéll in the wórld,
mén both lów and hígh,
rích and póor alíke!

My líps will speak wórds of wísdom.
My héart is fúll of ínsight.
I will túrn my mínd to a párable,
with the hárp I will sólve my próblem.

Whý should I féar in evil dáys
the málice of the fóes who surróund me,
mén who trúst in their wéalth,
and bóast of the vástness of their ríches?

For nó man can búy his own ránsom,
or pay a príce to Gód for his lífe.
The ránsom of his sóul is beyónd him.
He cánnot buy life without énd,
nor avóid cóming to the gráve.

He knows that wíse men and fóols must both pérish
and léave their wéalth to óthers.
Their gráves are their hómes for éver,
their dwélling place from áge to áge,
though their námes spread wíde through the lánd.

53

WEEK 2: TUESDAY

In his ríches, mán lacks wísdom:
hé is like the béasts that are destróyed.

Ant. You cannot serve both God and wealth.
Ant. 2: Store up treasure for yourselves in heaven, says the Lord.

II
This is the lót of those who trúst in themsélves,
who have óthers at their béck and cáll.
Like shéep they are dríven to the gráve,
where déath shall bé their shépherd
and the just shall becóme their rúlers.

With the mórning their óutward show vánishes
and the gráve becómes their hóme.
But Gód will ránsom me from déath
and táke my sóul to himsélf.

Then do not féar when a mán grows rich,
when the glóry of his hóuse incréases.
He takes nóthing wíth him when he dies,
his glóry does not fóllow him bélow.

Though he fláttered himsélf while he líved:
'Men will práise me for áll my succéss,'
yet he will gó to jóin his fáthers,
who will néver see the líght any móre.

In his ríches, mán lacks wísdom:
hé is like the béasts that are destróyed.

Ant. Store up treasure for yourselves in heaven, says the Lord.

SCRIPTURE READING   Rom 3:23–25a
Since all have sinned and fall short of the glory of God, they are justified by his grace as a gift, through the redemption which is in Christ Jesus, whom God put forward as an expiation by

his blood, to be received by faith. This was to show God's righteousness.

SHORT RESPONSORY

℟ You will give me the fulness of joy in your presence, O Lord.
Repeat ℟
℣ I will find happiness at your right hand for ever.

INTERCESSIONS

Christ is the shepherd of his flock: he loves and cares for his people. We turn to him in trust and say: ℟ Lord, we need your care.
Christ our Lord, you are pastor of all the ages, – protect our Bishop, N., and all the pastors of your Church. ℟
Be with those who are persecuted for their faith, and those cut off from the support of the Church: – Good Shepherd, in their pain and isolation may they know your care. ℟
Bring healing to the sick; – give nourishment to the hungry. ℟
We remember those who make our laws and those who apply them: – Lord, give them wisdom and discernment. ℟
Gather the flock for which you laid down your life: – bring home to their Father's house all who have died in your peace. ℟
Our Father

WEEK 2: WEDNESDAY

MORNING PRAYER

PSALMODY
Ant. 1: My heart exults in the Lord; he humbles and he exalts.

The poor rejoice in the Lord　　　Canticle: 1 Sam 2:1–10

He put down the mighty from their seats and exalted the lowly; he filled the hungry with good things (Lk 1:52–53)

> My heart exults in the Lord,
> I find my strength in my God;
> my mouth laughs at my enemies
> as I rejoice in your saving help.
> There is none like the Lord,
> there is none besides you.
> There is no Rock like our God.
>
> Bring your haughty words to an end,
> let no boasts fall from your lips,
> for the Lord is a God who knows all.
> It is he who weighs men's deeds.
>
> The bows of the mighty are broken,
> but the weak are clothed with strength.
> Those with plenty must labour for bread
> but the hungry need work no more.
> The childless wife has children now
> but the fruitful wife bears no more.

WEEK 2: WEDNESDAY

It is the Lord who gives life and death,
he brings men to the grave and back;
it is the Lord who gives poverty and riches.
He brings men low and raises them on high.

He lifts up the lowly from the dust,
from the ash heap he raises the poor
to set him in the company of princes,
to give him a glorious throne.

For the pillars of the earth are the Lord's,
on them he has set the world.
He guards the steps of his faithful,
but the wicked perish in darkness,
for no man's power gives him victory.
The enemies of the Lord shall be broken.

The Most High will thunder in the heavens,
the Lord will judge the ends of the earth.
He will give power to his king
and exalt the might of his anointed.

Ant. My heart exults in the Lord; he humbles and he exalts.

SCRIPTURE READING   Rom 8:35–37
Who will separate us from the love of Christ? Will affliction, or distress, or persecution, or hunger, or nakedness, or peril, or the sword? Yet in all this we are conquerors, through him who has granted us his love.

SHORT RESPONSORY
℞ I will praise the Lord at all times.
℣ His praise will be always on my lips.

WEEK 2: WEDNESDAY

INTERCESSORY

Nothing can separate us from the love of Christ, for he promised to be with his Church until the end of time. With confidence in his promise we pray: R⁷ Stay with us, Lord Jesus.

In all things we are victorious through your love: – take us into your care today. R⁷

Let the love of your Holy Spirit be in our hearts: – so that we may consecrate this day to you. R⁷

Help all Christians to answer your call: – may they be salt to the earth, and light to the world. R⁷

We pray for all those in industry: – may they work in harmony for justice and for the good of the whole community. R⁷

Our Father

EVENING PRAYER

PSALMODY

Ant. 1: The Lord will build a house for us; he will watch over our city.

Success depends on the Lord's blessing   Psalm 126 (127)

You are God's building (1 Cor 3:9)

If the Lórd does not buíld the hóuse,
in váin do its buílders lábour;
if the Lórd does not wátch over the cíty,
in váin does the wátchman keep vígil.

In váin is your éarlier rísing,
your góing láter to rést,
you who tóil for the bréad you éat:
when he pour gífts on his belóved while they slúmber.

Truly sóns are a gíft from the Lórd,
a bléssing, the frúit of the wómb.

WEEK 2: WEDNESDAY

Indéed the sóns of yóuth
are like árrows in the hánd of a wárrior.

Ó the háppiness of the mán
who has fílled his quíver with these árrows!
Hé will have no cáuse for sháme
when he dispútes with his fóes in the gáteways.

Ant. The Lord will build a house for us; he will watch over our city.
Ant. 2: He is the first-born of all creation; he is supreme over all creatures.

Christ is the first-born of all creation, the first-born from the dead
Canticle: Col 1:12–20

Let us give thanks to the Father,
who has qualified us to share
in the inheritance of the saints in light.

He has delivered us from the dominion of darkness
and transferred us to the kingdom of his beloved Son,
in whom we have redemption,
the forgiveness of sins.

He is the image of the invisible God,
the first-born of all creation,
for in him all things were created, in heaven and on earth,
visible and invisible.

All things were created
through him and for him.
He is before all things,
and in him all things hold together.

He is the head of the body, the Church;
he is the beginning,

the first-born from the dead,
that in everything he might be pre-eminent.

For in him all the fulness of God was pleased to dwell
and through him to reconcile to himself all things,
whether on earth or in heaven,
making peace by the blood of his cross.

Ant. He is the first-born of all creation; he is supreme over all creatures.

SCRIPTURE READING   1 Pet 5:5b–7
Wrap yourselves in humility to be servants of each other, because God refuses the proud and will always favour the humble. Bow down, then, before the power of God now, and he will raise you up on the appointed day; unload all your worries on to him, since he is looking after you.

SHORT RESPONSORY
℟ Guard us, Lord, as the apple of your eye.
℣ Hide us in the shadow of your wings.

INTERCESSIONS
At the end of the day we give thanks to God the Father who reconciled the whole universe to himself in Christ. ℟
Glory to you, Lord God!
We thank you for the beauty of creation: – may the work of man not disfigure it, but enhance it to your greater glory. ℟
We thank you, Father, for all the good things we enjoy: – teach us to be grateful and to use them well. ℟
Teach us to seek the things that please you, – then we shall find you in all that we do. ℟
Lord, as we journey towards the promised land, feed us with bread from heaven, – quench our thirst with living water. ℟

WEEK 2: WEDNESDAY

To you, a thousand years are like a single day: – take up those who have died with hope in you, and waken them into eternity. ℟
Our Father

WEEK 2: THURSDAY

MORNING PRAYER

PSALMODY

Ant. The Lord has done marvellous things, let them be made known to the whole world.

The rejoicing of a redeemed people   Canticle: Is 12:1–6

If any man is thirsty, let him come to me and drink (Jn 7:37)

> I thank you, Lord, you were angry with me
> but your anger has passed and you give me comfort.

> Truly, God is my salvation,
> I trust, I shall not fear.
> For the Lord is my strength, my song,
> he is my saviour.

> With joy you will draw water
> from the wells of salvation.
> Give thanks to the Lord, give praise to his name!
> Make his mighty deeds known to the peoples.

> Declare the greatness of his name,
> sing a psalm to the Lord!
> For he has done glorious deeds;
> make them known to all the earth.

> People of Sion, sing and shout for joy
> for great in your midst is the Holy One of Israel.

WEEK 2: THURSDAY

Ant. The Lord has done marvellous things, let them be made known to the whole world.

SCRIPTURE READING   Rom 14:17–19
The kingdom of God does not mean food and drink but righteousness and peace and joy in the Holy Spirit; he who thus serves Christ is acceptable to God and approved by men. Let us then pursue what makes for peace and for mutual upbuilding.

SHORT RESPONSORY
℟ Early in the morning I will think of you, O Lord.
℣ You have been my help.

INTERCESSIONS
Blessed be our God and Father: he hears the prayers of his children. ℟ Lord, hear us.
We thank you, Father, for sending us your Son: – let us keep him before our eyes throughout this day. ℟
Make wisdom our guide, – help us walk in newness of life. ℟
Lord, give us your strength in our weakness: – when we meet problems give us courage to face them. ℟
Direct our thoughts, our words, our actions today, – so that we may know, and do, your will. ℟
Our Father

WEEK 2: THURSDAY

EVENING PRAYER

PSALMODY

Ant. The Lord has given him power and honour and empire, and all peoples will serve him.

The judgment of God   Canticle: Rev 11:17–18; 12:10b–12a

> We give thanks to you, Lord God Almighty,
> who are and who were,
> that you have taken your great power
> and begun to reign.
>
> The nations raged,
> but your wrath came,
> and the time for the dead to be judged,
> for rewarding your servants, the prophets and saints,
> and those who fear your name,
> both small and great.
>
> Now the salvation and the power
> and the kingdom of our God
> and the authority of his Christ have come,
> for the accuser of our brethren has been thrown down,
> who accuses them day and night before our God.
>
> And they have conquered him
> by the blood of the Lamb
> and by the word of their testimony,
> for they loved not their lives even unto death.
> Rejoice then, O heaven,
> and you that dwell therein.

Ant. The Lord has given him power and honour and empire, and all peoples will serve him.

WEEK 2: THURSDAY

SCRIPTURE READING   1 Pet 1:22–23

You have been obedient to the truth and purified your souls until you can love like brothers, in sincerity; let your love for each other be real and from a pure heart – your new birth was not from any mortal seed but from the everlasting word of the living and eternal God.

SHORT RESPONSORY

℟ The Lord is my shepherd; there is nothing I shall want. Repeat ℟
℣ Fresh and green are the pastures where he gives me repose.

INTERCESSIONS

Let us lift up our hearts in thankfulness to God our Father, who has blessed us in Christ with every spiritual gift. ℟
Lord, bless your people.
Father, look on the Pope, our bishops, and all Christian leaders:
– sustain their faith, their love, and their courage. ℟
Almighty God, we pray for our country: – may it promote justice and brotherhood in the world. ℟
We pray for all who live the Christian life: – Father, look on them with kindness, and see in them the face of your beloved Son. ℟
Remember those who have consecrated themselves to serve you in the religious life: – enrich them in their poverty, love them in their chastity, lighten their hearts in obedience to you. ℟
Give rest to those who have died in Christ: – for with you there is mercy, and fulness of redemption. ℟
Our Father

Week 2: Friday

MORNING PRAYER

PSALMODY
Ant. In spite of your anger, Lord, have compassion.

God will appear in judgment   Canticle: Hab 3:2–4, 13a, 15–19

Lift up your heads, for your redemption is near at hand (Lk 21:28)

Lord, I have heard of your fame,
I stand in awe at your deeds.
Do them again in our days,
in our days make them known!
In spite of your anger, have compassion.

God comes forth from Teman,
the Holy One comes from Mount Paran.
His splendour covers the sky
and his glory fills the earth.
His brilliance is like the light,
rays flash from his hands;
there his power is hidden.

You march out to save your people,
to save the one you have anointed.
You made a path for your horses in the sea,
in the raging of the mighty waters.

This I heard and I tremble with terror,
my lips quiver at the sound.

Weakness invades my bones,
my steps fail beneath me
yet I calmly wait for the doom
that will fall upon the people who assail us.

For even though the fig does not blossom,
nor fruit grow on the vine,
even though the olive crop fail,
and fields produce no harvest,
even though flocks vanish from the folds
and stalls stand empty of cattle,

Yet I will rejoice in the Lord
and exult in God my saviour.
The Lord my God is my strength.
He makes me leap like the deer,
he guides me to the high places.

Ant. In spite of your anger, Lord, have compassion.

SCRIPTURE READING Eph 2:13–16
Now, in union with Christ Jesus, you who used to be far away have been brought near by the death of Christ. For Christ himself has brought us peace, by making the Jews and Gentiles one people. With his own body he broke down the wall that separated them and kept them enemies. He abolished the Jewish Law, with its commandments and rules, in order to create out of the two races one new people in union with himself, in this way making peace. By his death on the cross Christ destroyed the enmity; by means of the cross he united both races into one body and brought them back to God.

SHORT RESPONSORY
℟ I call to the Lord, the Most High, for he has been my help.
Repeat ℟
℣ May he send from heaven and save me.

WEEK 2: FRIDAY

INTERCESSIONS

Father, we praise you for your Son, our Lord Jesus Christ; through the Holy Spirit he offered himself in sacrifice to you, that we might be delivered from death and selfishness, and be free to live in your peace. R℣ Father, in your will is our peace.

We accept this new day as your gift, Lord; – grant that we may live in newness of life. R℣

You made all things, and keep all things in being; – give us the insight to see your hand at work in them all. R℣

Your Son sealed the new and everlasting covenant in his blood; – help us to live by this covenant and honour it. R℣

As Jesus died on the cross, blood and water flowed from his side; – as we share in the eucharist, pour out your Spirit upon us. R℣

Our Father

EVENING PRAYER

PSALMODY
Ant. 1: Lord, keep my soul from death, my feet from stumbling.

Thanksgiving Psalm 114 (116)

We must experience many hardships before we can enter the kingdom of God (Acts 14:22)

> I love the Lórd for hé has héard
> the crý of my appéal;
> for he túrned his éar to mé
> in the dáy when I cálled him.

WEEK 2: FRIDAY

They surróunded me, the snáres of déath,
with the ánguish of the tómb;
they cáught me, sórrow and distréss.
I called on the Lórd's name.

O Lórd my Gód, delíver me!

How grácious is the Lórd, and júst;
our Gód has compássion.
The Lórd protécts the simple héarts;
I was hélpless so he sáved me.

Turn báck, my sóul, to your rést
for the Lórd has been góod;
he has képt my sóul from déath,
my éyes from téars
and my féet from stúmbling.

I will wálk in the présence of the Lórd
in the lánd of the líving.

Ant. Lord, keep my soul from death, my feet from stumbling.
Ant. 2: My help shall come from the Lord who made heaven and earth.

God, the protector of his people   Psalm 120 (121)

They will never hunger or thirst again; neither the sun or scorching wind will ever plague them (Rev 7:16)

I líft up my éyes to the móuntains;
from whére shall come my hélp?
My hélp shall cóme from the Lórd
who made héaven and éarth.

May he néver állow you to stúmble!
Let him sléep not, your guárd.
Nó, he sléeps not nor slúmbers,
Ísrael's guárd.

WEEK 2: FRIDAY

The Lórd is your guárd and your sháde;
at your ríght side he stánds.
By dáy the sún shall not smíte you
nor the móon in the níght.

The Lórd will guárd you from évil,
he will guárd your sóul.
The Lord will guárd your góing and cóming
both nów and for éver.

Ant. My help shall come from the Lord who made heaven and earth.

SCRIPTURE READING   1 Cor 2:7–10a
The hidden wisdom of God which we teach in our mysteries is the wisdom that God predestined to be for our glory before the ages began. It is a wisdom that none of the masters of this age have ever known, or they would not have crucified the Lord of Glory; we teach what scripture calls: the things that no eye has seen and no ear has heard, things beyond the mind of man, all that God has prepared for those who love him. These are the very things that God has revealed to us through the Spirit.

SHORT RESPONSORY
℟ Christ died for our sins, that he might offer us to God.
Repeat ℟
℣ In the body he was put to death, in the spirit he was raised to life.

INTERCESSIONS
Christ comforted the widow who had lost her only son: let us pray to him, who will come at the last to wipe away every tear from our eyes. ℟ Come, Lord Jesus.
Lord Jesus, you consoled especially the poor and troubled: – look with mercy on those in any kind of need. ℟

WEEK 2: FRIDAY

The angel brought you the Father's comfort on the eve of your passion: – we pray that your comfort may strengthen those who are dying. ℟

Let all exiles know your care for them; – may they find their homelands once more, and come one day in joy to the Father's house. ℟

Look in love on all whose sins have separated them from you: – reconcile them to yourself and to your Church. ℟

The dead suffered the pain and loss of human life: – give them the fulness of life and joy in heaven. ℟

Our Father

Week 2: Saturday

MORNING PRAYER

PSALMODY
Ant. How great is your name, Lord, through all the earth!

The majesty of the Lord, the dignity of man Psalm 8

He has put all things under his feet, and appointed him to be head of the whole Church (Eph 1:22)

How gréat is your náme, O Lórd our Gód,
through áll the éarth!

Your májesty is práised above the héavens;
on the líps of chíldren and of bábes
you have found práise to fóil your énemy,
to sílence the fóe and the rébel.

When I see the héavens, the wórk of your hánds,
The móon and the stárs which you arránged,
what is mán that you should kéep him in mínd,
mortal mán that you cáre for hím?

Yet you have máde him little léss than a gód;
with glóry and hónour you crówned him,
gave him pówer over the wórks of your hánd,
put áll things únder his féet.

Áll of them, shéep and cáttle,
yes, éven the sávage béasts,
bírds of the aír, and físh
that máke their wáy through the wáters.

WEEK 2: SATURDAY

How gréat is your náme, O Lórd our Gód,
through áll the éarth!

Ant. How great is your name, Lord, through all the earth!

SCRIPTURE READING   Rom 12:14–16a
Bless those who persecute you; bless and do not curse them. Rejoice with those who rejoice, weep with those who weep. Live in harmony with one another; do not be haughty, but associate with the lowly.

SHORT RESPONSORY
℟ When I sing to you my lips shall rejoice.
℣ My tongue shall tell the tale of your justice.

INTERCESSIONS
God the Father has adopted us as brothers of his only Son, and through the ages has stayed with us and kept us in his love. Let us ask him for the needs of the world. ℟ Lord, help us as we work.

We pray for all who plan and build in our cities: – give them respect for every human value. ℟

Pour out your Spirit on artists, craftsmen, and musicians: – may their work bring variety, joy, and inspiration to our lives. ℟

Be with us as the cornerstone of all that we build: – for we can do nothing well without your aid. ℟

You have created us anew in the resurrection of your Son: – give us the strength to create a new life, and a new world. ℟

Our Father

WEEK 2: SATURDAY

EVENING PRAYER

PSALMODY
Ant. 2: I will take the chalice of salvation, and I will call on the name of the Lord.

Thanksgiving in the temple
Psalm 115 (116)

Through him (Christ), let us offer God an unending sacrifice of praise (Heb 13:15)

I trústed, éven when I sáid:
'I am sórely afflícted,'
and whén I said in my alárm:
'No mán can be trústed.'

How cán I repáy the Lórd
for his góodness to mé?
The cúp of salvátion I will ráise,
I will cáll on the Lórd's name.

My vóws to the Lórd I will fulfíl
befóre all his péople.
O précious in the éyes of the Lórd
is the déath of his fáithful.

Your sérvant, Lord, your sérvant am Í;
you have lóosened my bónds.
A thánksgiving sácrifice I máke:
I will cáll on the Lórd's name.

My vóws to the Lórd I will fulfíl
befóre all his péople,
in the cóurts of the hóuse of the Lórd,
in your mídst, O Jerúsalem.

Ant. I will take the chalice of salvation, and I will call on the name of the Lord.

Ant. 2: The Lord Jesus humbled himself, but God exalted him on high for ever.

Christ, the servant of God　　　　　　　　Canticle: Phil 2:6–11

> Though he was in the form of God,
> Jesus did not count equality with God a thing to be grasped.
>
> He emptied himself,
> taking the form of a servant,
> being born in the likeness of men.
>
> And being found in human form,
> he humbled himself and became obedient unto death,
> even death on a cross.
>
> Therefore God has highly exalted him
> and bestowed on him the name which is above every name,
>
> That at the name of Jesus every knee should bow,
> in heaven and on earth and under the earth,
>
> And every tongue confess that Jesus Christ is Lord,
> to the glory of God the Father.

Ant. The Lord Jesus humbled himself, but God exalted him on high for ever.

SCRIPTURE READING　　　　　　　　　　　　　　Heb 13:20–21
I pray that the God of peace, who brought our Lord Jesus back from the dead to become the great Shepherd of the sheep by the blood that sealed an eternal covenant, may make you ready to do his will in any kind of good action; and turn us all into whatever is acceptable to himself through Jesus Christ, to whom be glory for ever and ever, Amen.

WEEK 2: SATURDAY

SHORT RESPONSORY
℞ How great are your works, O Lord.
℣ In wisdom you have made them all.

INTERCESSIONS
Christ our Lord is mindful of all who need him, and does great things for love of them. Let us not be afraid to ask him for all our needs. ℞ Show us your loving kindness.

Lord, we know that the good things we have received today have come as a gift from you: – may we receive them with thankfulness and learn how to give. ℞

Saviour and light of all people, keep missionaries in your special care: – may the light of your Spirit burn strongly in them. ℞

Grant that the world may be filled with the knowledge of your truth; – help us to carry out all you have called us to do. ℞

You healed the sickness and pain of your brothers: – Bring healing and comfort to the spirit of man. ℞

Give rest to the faithful departed; – and bring them to praise you in eternity. ℞

Our Father

Week 3: Sunday

MORNING PRAYER

PSALMODY
Ant. Let us listen for the voice of the Lord and enter into his peace.

A call to praise God   Psalm 94 (95)

Every day, as long as this 'today' lasts, keep encouraging one another (Heb 3:13)

Come, ríng out our jóy to the Lórd;
háil the Gód who sáves us.
Let us cóme before him, gíving thánks,
with sóngs let us háil the Lórd.

A míghty Gód is the Lórd,
a gréat king abóve all góds.
In his hánd are the dépths of the éarth;
the héights of the móuntains are hís.
To hím belongs the séa, for he máde it,
and the drý land sháped by his hánds.

Come ín; let us bów and bend lów;
let us knéel before the Gód who máde us
for hé is our Gód and wé
the péople who belóng to his pásture,
the flóck that is léd by his hánd.

O that todáy you would lísten to his vóice!
'Hárden not your héarts as at Meríbah,

WEEK 3: SUNDAY

as on that dáy at Mássah in the désert
when your fáthers pút me to the tést;
when they tríed me, thóugh they saw my wórk.

For forty yéars I was wéaried of these péople
and I said: "Their héarts are astráy,
these péople do not knów my wáys."
Thén I took an óath in my ánger:
"Néver shall they énter my rést."'

Ant. Let us listen for the voice of the Lord and enter into his peace.

SCRIPTURE READING   Ezek 37:12b–14
The Lord God says this: I am now going to open your graves; I mean to raise you from your graves, my people, and lead you back to the soil of Israel. And you will know that I am the Lord, when I open your graves and raise you from your graves, my people. And I shall put my spirit in you, and you will live, and I shall resettle you on your own soil; and you will know that I, the Lord, have said and done this – it is the Lord God who speaks.

SHORT RESPONSORY
℟ You are the Christ, the Son of the living God. Have mercy on us.
℣ You are seated at the right hand of the Father.

INTERCESSIONS
We pray to the Father, who sent his Holy Spirit to bring new light to the hearts of us all. ℟ Lord, send us the light of your Spirit.
Blessed are you, the source of all light; – all creation rightly gives you praise. ℟

WEEK 3: SUNDAY

Through the resurrection of your Son, the world is filled with light: – through the gift of your Spirit, may your light shine out in the Church. ℟
Through your Holy Spirit, the disciples remembered all that Jesus taught them: – pour out your Spirit on the Church that she may be faithful to that teaching. ℟
Light of all the nations, look upon those who live in darkness: – open their hearts to accept you as the one true God. ℟
Our Father

EVENING PRAYER

PSALMODY
Ant 1. The Lord is full of merciful love; he makes us remember his wonders, alleluia.

Great are the works of the Lord Psalm 110 (111)

How great and wonderful are all your works, Lord God Almighty (Rev 15:3)

> I will thánk the Lórd with all my héart
> in the méeting of the júst and their assémbly.
> Gréat are the wórks of the Lórd;
> to be póndered by áll who lóve them.
>
> Majéstic and glórious his wórk,
> his jústice stands fírm for éver.
> He mákes us remémber his wónders.
> The Lórd is compássion and lóve.
>
> He gives fóod to thóse who féar him;
> keeps his cóvenant éver in mínd.
> He has shówn his míght to his péople
> by gíving them the lánds of the nátions.

WEEK 3: SUNDAY

His wórks are jústice and trúth:
his précepts are áll of them súre,
standing fírm for éver and éver:
they are máde in úprightness and trúth.

He has sént delíverance to his péople
and estáblished his cóvenant for éver.
Hóly his náme, to be féared.

To fear the Lórd is the fírst stage of wísdom;
all who dó so próve themselves wíse.
His práise shall lást for éver!

Ant. The Lord is full of merciful love; he makes us remember his wonders, alleluia.

Ant. 2: The Lord our God almighty is king, alleluia.

The marriage feast of the Lamb Canticle: Cf Rev 19:1–2, 5–7

Alleluia.
Salvation and glory and power belong to our God,
His judgments are true and just.
℟ Alleluia.

Alleluia.
Praise our God, all you his servants,
You who fear him, small and great.
℟ Alleluia.

Alleluia.
The Lord our God, the Almighty, reigns,
Let us rejoice and exult and give him the glory.
℟ Alleluia

Alleluia.
The marriage of the Lamb has come,
And his bride has made herself ready.
℟ Alleluia.

WEEK 3: SUNDAY

Ant. The Lord our God almighty is king, alleluia.

SCRIPTURE READING   1 Pet 1:3–5
Blessed be God the Father of our Lord Jesus Christ, who in his great mercy has given us a new birth as his sons, by raising Jesus Christ from the dead, so that we have a sure hope and the promise of an inheritance that can never be spoilt or soiled and never fade away, because it is being kept for you in the heavens. Through your faith, God's power will guard you until the salvation which has been prepared is revealed at the end of time.

SHORT RESPONSORY
℟ Blessed are you, O Lord, in the vault of heaven. Repeat ℟
℣ You are exalted and glorified above all else for ever. ℟

INTERCESSIONS
God is ever creative. His love renews all things and is the source of our hope. Let us turn to him in confidence: ℟ Lord, accept our thanks and our prayers.
We give thanks for the order of created things: – you have blessed us with the resources of the earth and the gift of human life. ℟
We give thanks for man's share in your continuing work of creation: – we praise you for your gifts to him of inventive skill and creative vision. ℟
We pray for all the nations of the world: – may those in authority work for peace and goodwill among men. ℟
We pray for all who are homeless today: – we pray for families searching for a place to live, and for refugees driven from their homeland. ℟
Life was your first gift to us: – may those who have died come to its fulness in you. ℟
Our Father

Week 3: Monday

MORNING PRAYER

PSALMODY
Ant. O sing to the Lord, bless his name.

The Lord is king and ruler of all the earth   Psalm 95 (96)

They were singing a new hymn in front of the throne, in the presence of the Lamb (Cf Rev 14:3)

O síng a new sóng to the Lórd,
síng to the Lórd all the éarth.
O síng to the Lórd, bless his náme.
Procláim his hélp day by dáy,
téll among the nátions his glóry
and his wónders amóng all the péoples.

The Lord is gréat and wórthy of práise,
to be féared abóve all góds;
the góds of the héathens are náught.

It was the Lórd who máde the héavens,
his are májesty and státe and pówer
and spléndour in his hóly pláce.

Give the Lórd, you fámilies of péoples,
give the Lórd glóry and pówer,
give the Lórd the glóry of his náme.

Bring an óffering and énter his cóurts,
wórship the Lórd in his témple.
O eárth, trémble befóre him.

WEEK 3: MONDAY

Procláim to the nátions: 'God is kíng.'
The wórld he made fírm in its pláce;
he will júdge the péoples in fáirness.

Let the héavens rejóice and earth be glád,
let the séa and all withín it thunder práise,
let the lánd and all it béars rejóice,
all the trées of the wóod shout for jóy

at the présence of the Lórd for he cómes,
he cómes to rúle the éarth.
With jústice he will rúle the wórld,
he will júdge the péoples with his trúth.

Ant. O sing to the Lord, bless his name.

SCRIPTURE READING   Jas 2:12–13
Talk and behave like people who are going to be judged by the law of freedom, because there will be judgment without mercy for those who have not been merciful themselves; but the merciful need have no fear of judgment.

SHORT RESPONSORY
℟ Blessed be the Lord from age to age.
℣ He alone has wrought marvellous works.

INTERCESSIONS
In the life of his incarnate Son, God has shown us the dignity of man's labour. With this in mind we pray: ℟ Lord, bless our work.
We bless you, Lord, for bringing us to this day; – we thank you for protecting our lives and giving us what we need. ℟
Be with us, Lord, as we take up our daily tasks: – and help us to remember that it is in your world we live and work. ℟
You have called us to serve you responsibly in the world: – help us to build a just and Christian society. ℟

WEEK 3: MONDAY

Stay with us and with everyone we meet this day: – let us give
your joy and your peace to the world. ℟
Our Father

EVENING PRAYER

PSALMODY
Ant. 1: Our help is in the name of the Lord, who made heaven
and earth.

Our help is in the name of the Lord Psalm 123 (124)

The Lord said to Paul, 'Do not fear; for I am with you'
(Acts 18:9–10)

'If the Lórd had not béen on our síde',
this is Ísrael's sóng.
'If the Lórd had not béen on our síde
when mén rose agáinst us,
thén would they have swállowed us alíve
when their ánger was kíndled.

Thén would the wáters have engúlfed us,
the tórrent gone óver us;
óver our héad would have swépt
the ráging wáters.'

Bléssed be the Lórd who did not gíve us
a préy to their téeth!
Our lífe, like a bírd, has escáped
from the snáre of the fówler.

Indéed the snáre has been bróken
and wé have escáped.
Our hélp is in the náme of the Lórd,
who made héaven and éarth.

Ant. Our help is in the name of the Lord, who made heaven and earth.
Ant. 2: God has chosen us to be his adopted children through his Son.

God, the Saviour Canticle: Eph 1:3–10

Blessed be the God and Father
of our Lord Jesus Christ,
who has blessed us in Christ
with every spiritual blessing in the heavenly places.

He chose us in him
before the foundation of the world,
that we should be holy
and blameless before him.

He destined us in love
to be his sons through Jesus Christ,
according to the purpose of his will,
to the praise of his glorious grace
which he freely bestowed on us in the Beloved.

In him we have redemption through his blood,
the forgiveness of our trespasses,
according to the riches of his grace
which he lavished upon us.

He has made known to us
in all wisdom and insight
the mystery of his will,
according to his purpose
which he set forth in Christ.

His purpose he set forth in Christ,
as a plan for the fulness of time,
to unite all things in him,
things in heaven and things on earth.

WEEK 3: MONDAY

Ant. God has chosen us to be his adopted children through his Son.

SCRIPTURE READING   Jas 4:11–12

Brothers, do not slander one another. Anyone who slanders a brother, or condemns him, is speaking against the Law and condemning the Law. But if you condemn the Law, you have stopped keeping it and become a judge over it. There is only one lawgiver and he is the only judge and has the power to acquit or to sentence. Who are you to give a verdict on your neighbour?

SHORT RESPONSORY

℟ Heal my soul for I have sinned against you.
℣ I said: 'Lord, have mercy on me.'

INTERCESSIONS

The will of Christ is for all men to be saved. Let us pray that his will may be done. ℟ Draw all men to yourself, Lord.

Lord, by your sacrifice on the cross you redeemed us from the slavery of sin: – lead us to the freedom and glory of the sons of God. ℟

Be with our bishop, N., and all the bishops of your Church: – grant them courage and compassion in their ministry. ℟

Help those who seek the truth to find it: – let them be consecrated in truth. ℟

We pray especially for peace in family life, and for those orphaned and widowed: – comfort them in your love. ℟

May our departed brothers and sisters come to the heavenly city: – there, with the Father and Holy Spirit, you will reign for ever. ℟

Our Father

Week 3: Tuesday

MORNING PRAYER

PSALMODY
Ant. 1: At night my soul longs for you; I watch for you at daybreak.

Hymn after victory over the enemy
Canticle: Is 26:1–4, 7–9, 12

The city walls stood on twelve foundation stones (cf Rev 21:14)

We have a strong city;
he sets up salvation as walls and bulwarks.
Open the gates
that the righteous nation which keeps faith may enter in.

You keep him in perfect peace,
whose mind is stayed on you,
because he trusts in you.
Trust in the Lord for ever,
for the Lord God is an everlasting rock.

The way of the righteous is level;
you make smooth the path of the righteous.
In the path of your judgments, O Lord,
we wait for you.

My soul yearns for you in the night,
my spirit within me earnestly seeks you;
for when your judgments are in the earth,
the inhabitants of the world learn righteousness.

WEEK 3: TUESDAY

O Lord, you will ordain peace for us;
you have wrought for us all our works.

Ant. At night my soul longs for you; I watch for you at daybreak.
Ant. 2: Lord, let your face shed its light upon us.

All the peoples will give praise to the Lord   Psalm 66 (67)

Let it be known to you that this salvation from God has been sent to all peoples (Acts 28:28)

O Gód, be grácious and bléss us
and let your fáce shed its líght upón us.
So will your wáys be knówn upon éarth
and all nátions learn your sáving hélp.

Let the péoples práise you, O Gód;
let áll the péoples práise you.

Let the nátions be glád and exúlt
for you rúle the wórld with jústice.
With fáirness you rúle the péoples,
you guide the nátions on éarth.

Let the péoples práise you, O Gód;
let áll the péoples práise you.

The éarth has yíelded its frúit
for Gód, our Gód, has bléssed us.
May Gód still gíve us his bléssing
till the énds of the éarth revére him.

Let the péoples práise you, O Gód;
let áll the péoples práise you.

Ant. Lord, let your face shed its light upon us.

WEEK 3: TUESDAY

SCRIPTURE READING   1 Jn 4:14-15

We ourselves saw and we testify
that the Father sent his Son
as saviour of the world.
If anyone acknowledges that Jesus is the Son of God,
God lives in him, and he in God.

SHORT RESPONSORY

℟ My helper is my God; I will place my trust in him.
℣ He is my refuge; he sets me free.

INTERCESSIONS

By shedding his blood for us, Christ gathered together a new people from every corner of the earth. Let us pray to him: ℟ Christ, be mindful of your people.
Christ, our king and redeemer: – help us to know your power and your love. ℟
Christ, our hope and courage: – sustain us throughout the day. ℟
Christ, our refuge and strength: – fight with us against our weakness. ℟
Christ, our joy and solace: – stay with the poor and lonely. ℟
Our Father

EVENING PRAYER

PSALMODY

Ant. 1: Unless you become like little children you will not enter the kingdom of heaven.

Childlike confidence in the Lord   Psalm 130 (131)

Learn from me, for I am gentle and humble in heart (Mt 11:29)

    O Lórd, my héart is not próud
    nor háughty my éyes.

WEEK 3: TUESDAY

> I have not góne after thíngs too gréat
> nor márvels beyónd me.
>
> Trúly I have sét my sóul
> in sílence and péace.
> As a chíld has rést in its mother's árms,
> even só my sóul.
>
> O Ísrael, hópe in the Lórd
> both nów and for éver.

Ant. Unless you become like little children you will not enter the kingdom of heaven.
Ant. 2: Lord, you made us a kingdom and priests to serve our God.

Hymn of the redeemed   Canticle: Rev 4:11; 5: 9, 10, 12

> Worthy are you, our Lord and God,
> to receive glory and honour and power,
> for you created all things,
> and by your will they existed and were created.
>
> Worthy are you, O Lord,
> to take the scroll and to open its seals,
> for you were slain,
> and by your blood you ransomed men for God
> from every tribe and tongue and people and nation.
>
> You have made us a kingdom and priests to our God,
> and we shall reign on earth.
>
> Worthy is the Lamb who was slain,
> to receive power and wealth,
> and wisdom and might,
> and honour and glory and blessing.

WEEK 3: TUESDAY

Ant. Lord, you made us a kingdom and priests to serve our God.

SCRIPTURE READING   Rom 12:9–12
Let love be genuine; hate what is evil, hold fast to what is good; love one another with brotherly affection; outdo one another in showing honour. Never flag in zeal, be aglow with the Spirit, serve the Lord. Rejoice in your hope, be patient in tribulation, be constant in prayer.

SHORT RESPONSORY
℟ Your word, O Lord, will endure for ever.
℣ Your truth will last from age to age.

INTERCESSIONS
God has established his people in hope. Nothing can break the confidence of those who love him. Let us proclaim: ℟ Father, our trust is in you.

We give you thanks, Lord God, – for you have made man rich in all wisdom and insight. ℟

Lord God, you know the hearts of all rulers: – may they work for the good of the people they govern. ℟

Lord, you empower mankind to glorify this world with art: – make our work live with vision and true hope. ℟

You do not allow us to be tempted beyond our limits: – strengthen the weak, raise up the fallen. ℟

Father, you have promised men a share in your Son's resurrection on the last day: – remember those who have gone before us on the path to eternal life. ℟

Our Father

Week 3: Wednesday

MORNING PRAYER

PSALMODY
Ant. Give joy to your servant, Lord, for to you I lift up my soul.

Prayer of a poor man in distress
Psalm 85 (86)

Blessed be God who comforts us in all our sorrows
(2 Cor 1:3–4)

> Turn your éar, O Lórd, and give ánswer
> for Í am póor and néedy.
> Preserve my lífe, for Í am fáithful;
> save the sérvant who trústs in yóu.
>
> You are my Gód, have mércy on me, Lórd,
> for I crý to you áll the day lóng.
> Give jóy to your sérvant, O Lórd,
> for to yóu I líft up my sóul.
>
> O Lórd, you are góod and forgíving,
> full of lóve to áll who cáll.
> Give héed, O Lórd, to my práyer
> and atténd to the sóund of my vóice.
>
> In the dáy of distréss I will cáll
> and súrely yóu will replý.
> Among the góds there is nóne like you, O Lórd;
> nor wórk to compáre with yoúrs.
>
> All the nátions shall cóme to adóre you
> and glórify your náme, O Lórd:

WEEK 3: WEDNESDAY

for you are gréat and do márvellous déeds,
yóu who alóne are Gód.

Shów me, Lórd, your wáy
so that Í may wálk in your trúth.
Guide my héart to féar your náme.

I will práise you, Lord my Gód, with all my héart
and glórify your náme for éver;
for your lóve to mé has been gréat:
you have sáved me from the dépths of the gráve.

The próud have rísen agáinst me;
rúthless men séek my lífe:
to yóu they páy no héed.

But yóu, God of mércy and compássion,
slów to ánger, O Lórd,
abóunding in lóve and trúth,
túrn and take píty on mé.

O gíve your stréngth to your sérvant
and sáve your hándmaid's són.
Shów me a sígn of your fávour
that my fóes may sée to their sháme
that you consóle me and gíve me your hélp.

Ant. Give joy to your servant, Lord, for to you I lift up my soul.

SCRIPTURE READING   Job 1:21; 2:10b

Naked I came from my mother's womb,
naked I shall return.
The Lord gave, the Lord has taken back.
Blessed be the name of the Lord!
If we take happiness from God's hand, must we not take sorrow
    too?

WEEK 3: WEDNESDAY

SHORT RESPONSORY
℟ Bend my heart to your will, O God.
℣ By your word, give me life.

INTERCESSIONS
God is love: he who dwells in love dwells in God, and God in him. In Jesus Christ we see how God loves us. Let us renew our faith in his love: ℟ Lord Jesus, you loved us and gave yourself for us.
You have given us life and light this morning: – let us give thanks for such great gifts. ℟
You are sole master of the future: – keep us from despair and the fear of what is to come. ℟
Love has no ambition to seek anything for itself: – strengthen our will to give up selfishness today. ℟
May your love in us overcome all things: – let there be no limit to our faith, our hope, and our endurance. ℟
Our Father

EVENING PRAYER

PSALMODY
Ant. 1: We are waiting in hope for the blessings of the glorious coming of our Saviour.

Peace in God   Psalm 61 (62)

May the God of hope fill you with all peace as you believe in him (Rom 15:13)

In God álone is my sóul at rést;
my hélp comes from hím.
He alóne is my róck, my strónghold,
my fórtress: I stand fírm.

How lóng will you áll attack one mán

WEEK 3: WEDNESDAY

to bréak him dówn,
as thóugh he were a tóttering wáll,
or a túmbling fénce?

Their plán is ónly to destróy:
they take pléasure in líes.
With their móuth they útter bléssing
but in their héart they cúrse.

In God alóne be at rést, my sóul;
for my hópe comes from hím.
He alóne is my róck, my strónghold,
my fórtress: I stand fírm.

In Gód is my sáfety and glóry,
the róck of my stréngth.
Take réfuge in Gód all you péople.
Trúst him at áll times.
Póur out your héarts befóre him
for Gód is our réfuge.

Cómmon folk are ónly a bréath,
gréat men an illúsion.
Pláced in the scáles, they rise;
they weigh léss than a bréath.

Dó not put your trúst in oppréssion
nor vain hópes on plúnder.
Dó not set your héart on ríches
even whén they incréase.

For Gód has sáid only óne thing:
only twó do I knów:
that to Gód alóne belongs pówer
and to yóu, Lord, lóve;
and that yóu repáy each mán
accórding to his déeds.

WEEK 3: WEDNESDAY

Ant. We are waiting in hope for the blessings of the glorious coming of our Saviour.

SCRIPTURE READING
Eph 3:20–21

To him who is able to do so much more than we can ever ask for, or even think of, by means of the power working in us: to God be the glory in the church and in Christ Jesus, for all time, for ever and ever! Amen.

SHORT RESPONSORY
℟ Redeem me, Lord, and show me your mercy.
℣ Do not cast me away with sinners.

INTERCESSIONS
I may have faith strong enough to move mountains: but if I have no love, I am nothing. With this in mind we pray: ℟ Lord, grant us your love.
Lord, sustain us as we build and grow towards you: – increase our faith as we work. ℟
We are assailed by doubts, and weighed down by uncertainties, – release our hearts, to journey towards you with hope. ℟
Love keeps no score of wrong, and does not gloat over evil: – help us to delight in the truth, and rejoice in your gifts to others. ℟
Confirm the pilgrim Church in the faith of the apostles: – help us to encourage each other, sharing our gifts. ℟
Bring those who have died in your peace to that knowledge which fulfils faith and answers hope, – grant them the fulness of your love. ℟
Our Father

Week 3: Thursday

Morning Prayer

PSALMODY
Ant. The Lord is coming in power; the prize of his victory is with him.

The Good Shepherd:
God most-high and all-wise Canticle: Is 40:10–17

Behold, I come quickly, and my reward is with me (Rev 22:12)

Behold, the Lord God comes with might,
and his arm rules for him;
behold, his reward is with him,
and his recompense before him.

He will feed his flock like a shepherd,
he will gather the lambs in his arms,
he will carry them in his bosom,
and gently lead those that are with young.

Who has measured the waters in the hollow of his hand
and marked off the heavens with a span,
enclosed the dust of the earth in a measure
and weighed the mountains in scales
and the hills in a balance?

Who has directed the Spirit of the Lord,
or as his counsellor has instructed him?
Whom did he consult for his enlightenment,
and who taught him the path of justice,

WEEK 3: THURSDAY

taught him knowledge,
and showed him the way of understanding?

Behold, the nations are like a drop from a bucket,
and are accounted as the dust on the scales;
behold, he takes up the isles
like fine dust.

Lebanon would not suffice for fuel,
nor are its beasts enough for a burnt offering.
All the nations are as nothing before him,
they are accounted by him as less than nothing and
  emptiness.

Ant. The Lord is coming in power; the prize of his victory is with him.

SCRIPTURE READING 1 Pet 4:10–11
Each of you has received a special grace, so, like good stewards responsible for all these different graces of God, put yourselves at the service of others. If you are a speaker, speak in words which seem to come from God; if you are a helper, help as though every action was done at God's orders; so that in everything God may receive the glory through Jesus Christ.

SHORT RESPONSORY
℟ I called with all my heart; Lord, hear me.
℣ I will keep your commandments.

INTERCESSIONS
We adore and praise our God who reigns above the heavens. He is the Lord of all things and before him all creation is as nothing.
℟ We adore you, our Lord and God.
Eternal Father, it is by your gift that we praise you: – the wonder of our making is only surpassed by the splendour and joy of our coming to life in Christ. ℟

WEEK 3: THURSDAY

Lord, be with us as we start a new day: – move our hearts to seek you and our wills to serve you. ℟
Deepen our awareness of your presence: – teach us reverence and love for all that you made. ℟
To know you is to love those you created: – let our lives and our work be of service to our brothers. ℟
Our Father

EVENING PRAYER

PSALMODY
Ant. He will conceal you with his wings; you will not fear the terror of the night.

In the shelter of the Most High Psalm 90 (91)

Behold, I have given you power to tread underfoot serpents and scorpions (Lk 10:19)

> He who dwélls in the shélter of the Most Hígh
> and abídes in the sháde of the Almíghty
> sáys to the Lórd: 'My réfuge,
> my strónghold, my Gód in whom I trúst!'
>
> It is hé who will frée you from the snáre
> of the fówler who séeks to destróy you;
> hé will concéal you with his pínions
> and únder his wíngs you will find réfuge.
>
> You will not féar the térror of the níght
> nor the árrow that flíes by dáy,
> nor the plágue that prówls in the dárkness
> nor the scóurge that lays wáste at nóon.

WEEK 3: THURSDAY

A thóusand may fáll at your síde,
tén thousand fáll at your right,
yóu, it will néver appróach;
his fáithfulness is búckler and shíeld.

Your éyes have ónly to lóok
to sée how the wícked are repáid,
yóu who have said: 'Lord, my réfuge!'
and have máde the Most Hígh your dwélling.

Upon yóu no évil shall fáll,
no plágue appróach where you dwéll.
For yóu has he commánded his ángels,
to kéep you in áll your wáys.

They shall béar you upón their hánds
lest you stríke your fóot against a stóne.
On the líon and the víper you will tréad
and trámple the young líon and the drágon.

Since he clíngs to me in lóve, I will frée him;
protéct him for he knóws my náme.
When he cálls I shall ánswer: 'I am wíth you.'
I will sáve him in distréss and give him glóry.

With léngth of lífe I will contént him;
I shall lét him see my sáving pówer.

Ant. He will conceal you with his wings; you will not fear the terror of the night.

SCRIPTURE READING   1 Pet 3:8–9
You should all agree among yourselves and be sympathetic; love the brothers, have compassion and be modest and humble. Never pay back one wrong with another, or an angry word with another one; instead, pay back with a blessing. That is what you are called to do, so that you inherit a blessing yourself.

WEEK 3: THURSDAY

SHORT RESPONSORY
℟ The Lord fed us with finest wheat.
℣ He filled us with honey from the rock.

INTERCESSIONS
Christ is the high priest of his people: it is in him that we come together to make our prayer to the Father of us all. ℟ Father, put new hearts within us.
We thank you for calling us into the Church: – bless us with constant faith, and make it a source of life for others. ℟
Lord, bless N., our Pope: – we pray that his faith may not fail, and that he may strengthen his brothers. ℟
Turn sinners back to you: – grant us a humble and contrite heart. ℟
Your Son knew what it was to be excluded from his homeland. – Be mindful of those who must live far from their family and country. ℟
Give eternal rest to the dead: – bring the whole Church together in heaven. ℟
Our Father

Week 3: Friday

MORNING PRAYER

PSALMODY
Ant. Against you alone have I sinned; Lord, have mercy on me.

O God have mercy on me Psalm 50 (51)

You must be made new in mind and spirit, and put on the new nature (Eph 4:23–24)

Have mércy on me, Gód, in your kíndness.
In your compássion blot óut my offénce.
O wásh me more and móre from my guílt
and cléanse me fróm my sín.

My offénces trúly I knów them;
my sín is álways befóre me.
Against yóu, you alóne, have I sinned;
what is évil in your síght I have dóne.

That you may be jústified whén you give séntence
and be withóut repróach when you júdge,
O sée, in guílt I was born,
a sínner was I concéived.

Indéed you love trúth in the héart;
then in the sécret of my héart teach me wisdom.
O púrify me, thén I shall be cléan;
O wásh me, I shall be whíter than snów.

Make me héar rejóicing and gládness,
that the bónes you have crúshed may revíve.
From my síns turn awáy your fáce
and blót out áll my guílt.

A púre heart créate for me, O Gód,
put a stéadfast spírit withín me.
Do not cást me awáy from your présence,
nor deprive me of your hóly spírit.

Give me agáin the jóy of your hélp;
with a spírit of férvour sustáin me,
that I may téach transgréssors your wáys
and sínners may retúrn to yóu.

O réscue me, Gód, my hélper,
and my tóngue shall ríng out your góodness.
O Lórd, ópen my líps,
and my móuth shall decláre your práise.

For in sácrifice you táke no delíght,
burnt óffering from mé you would refúse,
my sácrifice, a cóntrite spírit.
A húmbled, contrite héart you will not spúrn.

In your góodness, show fávour to Síon:
rebuíld the wálls of Jerúsalem.
Thén you will be pléased with lawful sácrifice,
hólocausts óffered on your áltar.

Ant. Against you alone have I sinned; Lord, have mercy on me.

SCRIPTURE READING 2 Cor 12:9b–10
I am most happy, then, to be proud of my weaknesses, in order to feel the protection of Christ's power over me. I am content with

WEEK 3: FRIDAY

weaknesses, insults, hardships, persecutions, and difficulties for Christ's sake. For when I am weak, then I am strong.

SHORT RESPONSORY
℞ In the morning let me know your love.
℣ Make me know the way I should walk.

INTERCESSIONS
We have a high priest, able to sympathize with us in our weakness, one who, because of his likeness to us, has been tempted in every way, but did not sin. Let us pray to him: ℞ Show us your mercy and compassion.
Lord, for the joy which lay in the future, you willingly went to the cross: – make us share your death, that we may also share your joy. ℞
Lord, you said 'Let any man who thirsts come to me and drink': – give your Spirit now to those who thirst for you. ℞
You sent your disciples to preach the gospel to every nation: – bless those men and women who devote their lives to preaching the gospel today. ℞
Help those in pain to know that the Father cares for them – for he loves them as he loves his own Son. ℞
Our Father

WEEK 3: FRIDAY

EVENING PRAYER

PSALMODY
Ant. 1: The Lord is king, let earth rejoice.

The glory of the Lord's rule   Psalm 96 (97)

This psalm tells of the salvation of the world and of the faith all peoples would have in Christ (St Athanasius)

The Lórd is kíng, let éarth rejóice,
let áll the cóastlands be glád.
Clóud and dárkness are his ráiment;
his thróne, jústice and ríght.

A fíre prepáres his páth;
it búrns up his fóes on every síde.
His líghtnings líght up the wórld,
the éarth trémbles at the síght.

The móuntains mélt like wáx
before the Lórd of áll the éarth.
The skíes procláim his jústice;
all péoples sée his glóry.

Let thóse who serve ídols be ashámed,
those who bóast of their wórthless góds.
All you spírits, wórship hím.

Síon héars and is glád;
the péople of Júdah rejóice
becáuse of your júdgments O Lórd.

For yóu indéed are the Lórd
most hígh above áll the éarth
exálted far abóve all spírits.

WEEK 3: FRIDAY

The Lórd loves thóse who hate évil:
he guárds the sóuls of his sáints;
he séts them frée from the wícked.

Líght shines fórth for the júst
and jóy for the úpright of héart.
Rejóice, you júst, in the Lórd;
give glóry to his hóly náme.

Ant. The Lord is king, let earth rejoice.
Ant. 2: All peoples will come and adore you, Lord.

Hymn of adoration

Canticle: Rev 15:3–4

Great and wonderful are your deeds,
O Lord God the Almighty!
Just and true are your ways,
O King of the ages!

Who shall not fear and glorify your name, O Lord?
For you alone are holy.
All nations shall come and worship you,
for your judgments have been revealed.

Ant. All peoples will come and adore you, Lord.

SCRIPTURE READING Jas 1:2–4
My brothers! Consider yourselves fortunate when all kinds of trials come your way, because you know that when your faith succeeds in facing such trials, the result is the ability to endure. Be sure that your endurance carries you all the way, without failing, so that you may be perfect and complete, lacking nothing.

WEEK 3: FRIDAY

SHORT RESPONSORY
℟ Christ loved us and has washed away our sins with his blood.
℣ He made us a line of kings, priests to serve God.

INTERCESSIONS
Father, Christ prayed that we be forgiven through his passion. As you accepted him, accept his prayer for all sinners. ℟
Father, into your hands I commend my spirit.
Through his beloved disciple, Jesus gave us Mary to be our mother; – with her we pray to you for all her children. ℟
Father, heed the anguish of those who cry out to you with your Son: – 'My God, my God, why have you forsaken me?' ℟
Help us to hear the cry, 'I thirst'; – help us to see your Son, even in the least of his brothers. ℟
To the man dying with him, Jesus said, 'Truly I say to you, this day you will be with me in Paradise.' – Father, let these words be heard again by those who die tonight. ℟
We pray for those who have gone before us, signed with the sign of the cross: – may they rise with Christ in power when his voice resounds again through the universe: 'It is consummated.' ℟
Our Father

Week 3: Saturday

MORNING PRAYER

PSALMODY
Ant. To you our praise is due in Sion, O God.

Solemn thanksgiving   Psalm 64 (65)

Sion is to be understood as the heavenly city (Origen)

> To yóu our práise is dúe
> in Síon, O Gód.
> To yóu we páy our vóws,
> you who héar our práyer.
>
> To yóu all flésh will cóme
> with its búrden of sín.
> Too héavy for ús, our offénces,
> but you wípe them awáy.
>
> Blessed is hé whom you chóose and cáll
> to dwéll in your cóurts.
> We are fílled with the bléssings of your hóuse,
> of your hóly témple.
>
> You kéep your plédge with wónders,
> O Gód our sáviour,
> the hópe of áll the éarth
> and of fár distant ísles.
>
> You uphóld the móuntains with your stréngth,
> you are gírded with pówer.
> You stíll the róaring of the séas,

WEEK 3: SATURDAY

the róaring of their wáves
and the túmult of the péoples.

The énds of the éarth stand in áwe
at the síght of your wónders.
The lánds of súnrise and súnset
you fíll with your jóy.

You cáre for the earth, give it wáter,
you fíll it with ríches.
Your ríver in héaven brims óver
to províde its gráin.

And thús you províde for the éarth;
you drénch its fúrrows,
you lével it, sóften it with shówers,
you bléss its grówth.

You crówn the yéar with your góodness.
Abúndance flóws in your stéps,
in the pástures of the wílderness it flóws.

The hílls are gírded with jóy,
the méadows cóvered with flócks,
the válleys are décked with whéat.
They shoút for jóy, yes, they síng.

Ant. To you our praise is due in Sion, O God.

SCRIPTURE READING   Phil 2:14–15
Do everything without complaining or arguing, so that you may be innocent and pure, as God's perfect children who live in a world of corrupt and sinful people. You must shine among them like stars lighting up the sky.

WEEK 3: SATURDAY

SHORT RESPONSORY
℟ I called to you, Lord, you are my refuge.
℣ You are all I have in the land of the living.

INTERCESSIONS
From all eternity God chose Mary to be Mother of Christ. Therefore she is above all other creatures both in heaven and on earth. With her we proclaim: ℟ My soul glorifies the Lord.

Father, your Son Jesus gave his mother to the Church, a perfect example of faith: – may we accept your word in faith, as she did. ℟

Mary listened to your voice, and brought your Word into the world: – by answering your call, may we too bring your Son to men. ℟

You strengthened Mary to stand at the foot of the cross and filled her with joy at the resurrection: – by her intercession, lighten our sorrow and reinforce our hope. ℟

Our Father

WEEK 3: SATURDAY

EVENING PRAYER

PSALMODY
Ant. 1: From the rising of the sun to its setting, great is the name of the Lord.

Praised be the name of the Lord Psalm 112 (113)

He put down princes from their thrones and exalted the lowly (Lk 1:52)

Práise, O sérvants of the Lórd,
práise the náme of the Lórd!
May the náme of the Lórd be bléssed
both nów and for évermóre!
From the rísing of the sún to its sétting
práised be the náme of the Lórd!

Hígh above all nátions is the Lórd,
abóve the héavens his glóry.
Whó is like the Lórd, our Gód,
who has rísen on hígh to his thróne
yet stóops from the héights to look dówn,
to look dówn upon héaven and éarth?

From the dúst he lífts up the lówly,
from his mísery he ráises the póor
to sét him in the cómpany of prínces,
yés, with the prínces of his péople.
To the chíldless wífe he gives a hóme
and gláddens her héart with chíldren.

Ant. From the rising of the sun to its setting, great is the name of the Lord.
Ant. 2: The Lord Jesus humbled himself, but God exalted him on high for ever.

WEEK 3: SATURDAY

Christ, the servant of God Canticle: Phil 2:6–11

Though he was in the form of God,
Jesus did not count equality with God a thing to be grasped.

He emptied himself,
taking the form of a servant,
being born in the likeness of men.

And being found in human form,
he humbled himself and became obedient unto death,
even death on a cross.

Therefore God has highly exalted him
and bestowed on him the name which is above every name,

That at the name of Jesus every knee should bow,
in heaven and on earth and under the earth,

And every tongue confess that Jesus Christ is Lord,
to the glory of God the Father.

Ant. The Lord Jesus humbled himself, but God exalted him on high for ever.

SCRIPTURE READING   2 Pet 1:19–20
So we are even more confident of the message proclaimed by the prophets. You will do well to pay attention to it, because it is like a lamp shining in a dark place, until the Day dawns and the light of the morning star shines in your hearts. Above all else, however, remember this: no one can explain, by himself, a prophecy in the Scriptures. For no prophetic message ever came from the will of man, but men were carried along by the Holy Spirit as they spoke the message that came from God.

WEEK 3: SATURDAY

SHORT RESPONSORY
℟ From the rising of the sun to its setting, great is the name of the Lord.
℣ High above the heavens is his glory.

INTERCESSIONS
Let us pray to Christ, who, of his fulness, gives his brothers love in return for love. ℟ Lord Jesus, hear our prayer.
Firstborn from the dead, you have cleansed us of our sins by your blood. – Lead us to understand what you have done for us. ℟
You have called us to be heralds of the good news: – help us to enter the depths of its message and to make it our own. ℟
King of peace, guide the actions of those who govern: – may your Spirit move them to care for those whom society rejects. ℟
Guide the steps of those who are oppressed, those persecuted for race, colour, or religion: – let their dignity be respected, and their rights upheld. ℟
Welcome all who have died in your peace; – bring them to everlasting life with our Lady and all the saints. ℟
Our Father

Week 4: Sunday

MORNING PRAYER

PSALMODY
Ant. Give thanks to the Lord, for his great love is without end, alleluia.

Song of rejoicing in salvation   Psalm 117 (118)

This is the stone which was rejected by you builders, but which has become the cornerstone (Acts 4:11)

> Give thánks to the Lórd for he is góod,
> for his lóve endures for éver.
>
> Let the sóns of Ísrael sáy:
> 'His lóve endures for éver.'
> Let the sóns of Áaron sáy:
> 'His lóve endures for éver.'
> Let thóse who fear the Lórd sáy:
> 'His lóve endures for éver.'
>
> I cálled to the Lórd in my distréss;
> he ánswered and fréed me.
> The Lórd is at my síde; I do not féar.
> What can mán do agáinst me?
> The Lórd is at my síde as my helper:
> I shall look dówn on my fóes.

WEEK 4: SUNDAY

It is bétter to take réfuge in the Lórd
than to trúst in men:
it is bétter to take réfuge in the Lórd
than to trúst in prínces.

The nátions áll encómpassed me;
in the Lórd's name I crúshed them.
They cómpassed me, cómpassed me abóut;
in the Lórd's name I crúshed them.
They cómpassed me abóut like bées;
they blázed like a fíre among thórns.
In the Lórd's name I crúshed them.

I was hárd-préssed and was fálling
but the Lórd came to hélp me.
The Lórd is my stréngth and my sóng;
hé is my sáviour.

There are shóuts of jóy and víctory
in the ténts of the júst.

The Lórd's right hánd has tríumphed;
his ríght hand ráised me.
The Lórd's right hánd has tríumphed;
I shall not díe, I shall líve
and recóunt his déeds.
I was púnished, I was púnished by the Lórd,
but nót doomed to díe.

Ópen to mé the gates of hóliness:
I will énter and give thánks.
Thís is the Lórd's own gáte
where the júst may énter.
I will thánk you for yóu have ánswered
and yóu are my sáviour.

The stóne which the buílders rejécted
has becóme the córner stone.

115

WEEK 4: SUNDAY

> Thís is the wórk of the Lórd,
> a márvel in our éyes.
> Thís day was máde by the Lórd;
> we rejóice and are glád.
>
> O Lórd, gránt us salvátion;
> O Lórd, grant succéss.
> Bléssed in the náme of the Lórd
> is hé who cómes.
> We bléss you from the hóuse of the Lórd;
> the Lórd Gód is our líght.
>
> Go fórward in procéssion with bránches
> éven to the áltar.
> Yóu are my Gód, I thánk you.
> My Gód, I práise you.
> Give thánks to the Lórd for he is góod;
> for his lóve endures for éver.

Ant. Give thanks to the Lord, for his great love is without end, alleluia.

SCRIPTURE READING   2 Tim 2:8, 11–13

Remember the Good News that I carry, 'Jesus Christ is risen from the dead, sprung from the race of David.'
Here is a saying that you can rely on:
If we have died with him, then we shall live with him.
If we hold firm, then we shall reign with him.
If we disown him, then he will disown us.
We may be unfaithful, but he is always faithful,
for he cannot disown his own self.

SHORT RESPONSORY
℟ We give thanks to you, O God, and call upon your name.
℣ We recount your wonderful deeds.

WEEK 4: SUNDAY

INTERCESSIONS

To the only God, our Saviour, through Jesus Christ our Lord, be glory, majesty, dominion, and authority, before all time, now, and for ever. ℟ We praise you, O God: we acknowledge you to be the Lord.

We bless you, Lord, creator of the universe: we were sinners, in need of your grace: – yet now you have called us to live in knowledge and service of you. ℟

Your Son has shown us the way. – As we follow in his steps, may we never wander from the path that leads to life. ℟

We celebrate today the resurrection of your Son: – in suffering and in gladness, may it bring us deep joy. ℟

O Lord, give us the spirit of prayer and praise: – let us always and everywhere give you thanks. ℟

Our Father

EVENING PRAYER

PSALMODY
Ant. 1: Whoever eats this bread will live for ever, alleluia.

The Good Shepherd   Psalm 22 (23)

The Lamb is their king who leads them to the source of the water of life (Rev 7:17)

The Lórd is my shépherd;
there is nóthing I shall wánt.
Frésh and gréen are the pástures
where he gíves me repóse.
Near réstful wáters he léads me,
To revíve my drooping spírit.

He guídes me alóng the right páth;
he is trúe to his náme.

WEEK 4: SUNDAY

If I should wálk in the válley of dárkness
no évil would I féar.
You are thére with your cróok and your stáff;
with thése you give me cómfort.

You have prepáred a bánquet for mé
in the síght of my fóes.
My héad you have anóinted with óil;
my cúp is overflówing.

Surely góodness and kíndness shall fóllow me
all the dáys of my lífe.
In the Lórd's own house shall I dwéll
for éver and éver.

Ant. Whoever eats this bread will live for ever, alleluia.
Ant. 2: My spirit exults in the Lord God, my saviour.

The Canticle of Mary   Lk 1:46–55

My soul rejoices in the Lord

My soul glorifies the Lord,
my spirit rejoices in God, my Saviour.
He looks on his servant in her lowliness;
henceforth all ages will call me blessed.

The Almighty works marvels for me.
Holy his name!
His mercy is from age to age,
on those who fear him.

He puts forth his arm in strength
and scatters the proud-hearted.
He casts the mighty from their thrones
and raises the lowly.

He fills the starving with good things,
sends the rich away empty.

He protects Israel, his servant,
remembering his mercy,
the mercy promised to our fathers,
to Abraham and his sons for ever.

Ant. My spirit exults in the Lord God, my saviour.

SCRIPTURE READING   Heb 12:22–24
What you have come to is Mount Zion and the city of the living God, the heavenly Jerusalem where the millions of angels have gathered for the festival, with the whole Church in which everyone is a 'first-born son' and a citizen of heaven. You have come to God himself, the supreme Judge, and been placed with spirits of the saints who have been made perfect; and to Jesus, the mediator who brings a new covenant and a blood for purification which pleads more insistently than Abel's.

SHORT RESPONSORY
℟ Great is our Lord; great is his might.
℣ His wisdom can never be measured.

INTERCESSIONS
In the Church, God has made known to us his hidden purpose: to make all things one in Christ. Let us pray that his will may be done. ℟ Father, unite all things in Christ.
We give you thanks for the presence and power of your Spirit in the Church: – give us the will to search for unity, and inspire us to pray and work together. ℟
We give you thanks for all whose work proclaims your love: – help us to serve the communities in whose life we share. ℟
Father, care for all who serve in the Church as ministers of your word and sacraments: – may they bring your whole family to the unity for which Christ prayed. ℟

WEEK 4: SUNDAY

Your people have known the ravages of war and hatred: – grant that they may know the peace left by your Son. ℟
Fulfil the hopes of those who sleep in your peace: – bring them to that final resurrection when you will be all in all. ℟
Our Father

WEEK 4: MONDAY

MORNING PRAYER

PSALMODY
Ant. In the morning, Lord, you fill us with your love.

Let the splendour of the Lord come upon us
Psalm 89 (90)

With the Lord one day is like a thousand years, and a thousand years is like a day (2 Pet 3:8)

O Lórd, you have béen our réfuge
from óne generátion to the néxt.
Befóre the móuntains were bórn
or the éarth or the wórld brought fórth,
you are Gód, without begínning or énd.

You túrn men báck into dúst
and say: 'Go báck, sóns of mén.'
To yóur eyes a thóusand yéars
are like yésterday, cóme and góne,
no móre than a wátch in the níght.

You swéep men awáy like a dréam,
like gráss which springs úp in the mórning.
In the mórning it springs úp and flówers:
by évening it wíthers and fádes.

WEEK 4: MONDAY

So wé are destróyed in your ánger
strúck with térror in your fúry.
Our guílt lies ópen befóre you;
our sécrets in the líght of your fáce.

All our dáys pass awáy in your ánger.
Our lífe span is óver like a sígh.
Our spán is séventy yéars
or éighty for thóse who are stróng.

And most of thése are émptiness and páin.
They pass swíftly and wé are góne.
Who understánds the pówer of your ánger
and féars the stréngth of your fúry?

Make us knów the shórtness of our lífe
that we may gáin wísdom of héart.
Lord, relént! Is your ánger for éver?
Show píty tó your sérvants.

In the mórning, fíll us with your lóve;
we shall exúlt and rejóice all our dáys.
Give us jóy to bálance our afflíction
for the yéars when we knéw misfórtune.

Show fórth your wórk to your sérvants;
let your glóry shíne on their chíldren.
Let the fávour of the Lórd be upón us:
give succéss to the wórk of our hánds,
give succéss to the wórk of our hánds.

Ant. In the morning, Lord, you fill us with your love.

SCRIPTURE READING   Jud 8:21b–23
Remember that our fathers were put to the test to prove their love of God. Remember how our father Abraham was tested and became the friend of God after many trials and tribulations.

WEEK 4: MONDAY

The same was true of Isaac, Jacob, Moses, and all those who met with God's favour. They remained steadfast in the face of tribulations of every kind.

SHORT RESPONSORY
℟ Rejoice in the Lord, O you just; for praise is fitting for loyal hearts.
℣ Sing to him a new song.

INTERCESSIONS
Almighty Father, the heavens cannot hold your greatness: yet through your Son we have learned to say: ℟ Father, may your kingdom come!
We praise you as your children; – may your name be kept holy in the hearts of all mankind. ℟
Help us to live in the hope of heaven today: – make us ready to do your will on earth. ℟
Give us this day the courage to forgive others: – as you forgive us our trespasses. ℟
Father, be with us in all our trials: – do not allow us to fall away from you. ℟
Our Father

EVENING PRAYER

PSALMODY
Ant. Bless the Lord through the night.

Evening prayer in the temple   Psalm 133 (134)

Praise our God, all you his servants, and all who revere him, both great and small (Rev 19:5)

O cóme, bléss the Lórd,
all yóu who sérve the Lórd,

WEEK 4: MONDAY

> who stánd in the hóuse of the Lórd,
> in the cóurts of the hóuse of our Gód.
>
> Lift up your hánds to the hóly pláce
> and bléss the Lórd through the níght.
>
> May the Lórd bléss you from Síon,
> he who máde both héaven and éarth.

Ant. Bless the Lord through the night.
Ant. 2: All things were created in him, and he holds all things in being.

**Christ is the firstborn of all creation,
the firstborn from the dead**   Canticle: Col 1:12–20

> Let us give thanks to the Father,
> who has qualified us to share
> in the inheritance of the saints in light.
>
> He has delivered us from the dominion of darkness
> and transferred us to the kingdom of his beloved Son,
> in whom we have redemption,
> the forgiveness of sins.
>
> He is the image of the invisible God,
> the firstborn of all creation,
> for in him all things were created, in heaven and on earth,
> visible and invisible.
>
> All things were created
> through him and for him.
> He is before all things,
> and in him all things hold together.

WEEK 4: MONDAY

He is the head of the body, the Church;
he is the beginning,
the firstborn from the dead,
that in everything he might be pre-eminent.

For in him all the fulness of God was pleased to dwell,
and through him to reconcile to himself all things,
whether on earth or in heaven,
making peace by the blood of his cross.

Ant. All things were created in him, and he holds all things in being.

SCRIPTURE READING   1 Thess 3:12–13
May the Lord be generous in increasing your love and make you love one another and the whole human race as much as we love you. And may he so confirm your hearts in holiness that you may be blameless in the sight of our God and Father when our Lord Jesus Christ comes with all his saints.

SHORT RESPONSORY
℟ Let my prayer come before you, O Lord.
℣ Let it rise in your presence like incense.

INTERCESSIONS
Let us pray to God who never deserts those who trust in him. ℟
Lord, in your mercy, hear our prayer.
Pour out your Spirit on the Church; – let men see in her the greatness of your loving kindness. ℟
Be with the priests and ministers of your Church: – what they preach to others, may they practise in their lives. ℟
Teach us to understand one another more deeply: – by your presence, free us from prejudice and fear. ℟

WEEK 4: MONDAY

Give married couples constancy and mutual understanding: – may their difficulties help to deepen the love they have for each other. ℟

Pardon the sins of all our departed brothers and sisters: – may they enjoy new life in the company of your saints. ℟

Our Father

Week 4: Tuesday

Morning Prayer

PSALMODY
Ant. 1: My soul, give thanks to the Lord and never forget all his blessings.

Praise of the God of merciful love Psalm 102 (103)

Through the tender mercy of God, the Rising Sun has come to visit us from on high (cf Lk 1:78)

I
My sóul, give thánks to the Lórd,
all my béing, bléss his holy náme,
My sóul, give thánks to the Lórd,
and néver forgét all his bléssings.

It is hé who forgíves all your guílt,
who héals every óne of your ílls,
who redéems your lífe from the grave,
who crówns you with lóve and compássion,
who fílls your lífe with good thíngs,
renéwing your yóuth like an éagle's.

The Lórd does déeds of jústice,
gives júdgment for áll who are oppréssed.
He made knówn his wáys to Móses
and his déeds to Ísrael's sóns.

Ant. My soul, give thanks to the Lord and never forget all his blessings.

WEEK 4: TUESDAY

Ant. 2: As a father has compassion on his sons, the Lord has pity on those who fear him.

II
The Lórd is compássion and lóve,
slow to ánger and rích in mércy.
His wráth will cóme to an énd;
he will nót be ángry for éver.
He does not tréat us accórding to our síns
nor répay us accórding to our fáults.

For as the héavens are hígh above the éarth
so stróng is his lóve for those who féar him.
As fár as the éast is from the wést
so fár does he remóve our síns.

As a fáther has compássion on his sóns,
the Lord has píty on thóse who féar him;
for he knóws of whát we are máde,
he remémbers that wé are dúst.

As for mán, his dáys are like gráss;
he flówers like the flówer of the fíeld;
the wind blóws and hé is góne
and his pláce never sées him agáin.

Ant. As a father has compassion on his sons, the Lord has pity on those who fear him.
Ant. Give thanks to the Lord, all his works.

III
But the lóve of the Lórd is everlásting
upon thóse who hóld him in féar;
his jústice reaches óut to children's chíldren
when they kéep his cóvenant in trúth,
when they kéep his wíll in their mínd.

WEEK 4: TUESDAY

The Lórd has set his swáy in héaven
and his kíngdom is rúling over áll.
Give thánks to the Lórd, all his ángels,
mighty in pówer, fulfílling his wórd,
who héed the vóice of his wórd.

Give thánks to the Lórd, all his hósts,
his sérvants who dó his wíll.
Give thánks to the Lórd, all his wórks,
in évery pláce where he rúles.
My sóul, give thánks to the Lórd!

Ant. Give thanks to the Lord, all his works.

SCRIPTURE READING   Is 55:1
Oh, come to the water all you who are thirsty;
though you have no money, come!
Buy corn without money, and eat,
and, at no cost, wine and milk.

SHORT RESPONSORY
℟ Hear my cry, Lord, for I hope in your word.
℣ I rise before dawn and call for help.

INTERCESSIONS
Our sufferings bring acceptance, acceptance brings hope: and our hope will not deceive us, for the Spirit has been poured into our hearts. It is through the same Spirit that we pray: ℟ Stay with us, Lord, on our journey.
Help us to realize that our troubles are slight and shortlived; – they are as nothing compared with the joy we shall have when we reach our home with you. ℟
Come to the lonely, the unloved, those without friends; – show them your love, and help them to care for their brothers and sisters. ℟

WEEK 4: TUESDAY

Take away our pride, temper our anger: – may we follow you in your gentleness: may you make us humble of heart. ℟
Give us the fulness of your Spirit, the Spirit of sonship: – make our love for each other generous and sincere. ℟
Our Father

EVENING PRAYER

PSALMODY
Ant. 1: Before the angels I will bless you, my God.

Thanksgiving   Psalm 137 (138)

The kings of the earth will bring glory and honour to the holy city (cf Rev 21:24)

I thánk you, Lórd, with all my héart,
you have héard the wórds of my móuth.
In the présence of the ángels I will bléss you.
I will adóre before your hóly témple.

I thánk you for your fáithfulness and lóve
which excél all we éver knew of yóu.
On the dáy I cálled, you ánswered;
you incréased the stréngth of my sóul.

Áll earth's kíngs shall thánk you
when they héar the wórds of your móuth.
They shall síng of the Lórd's wáys:
'How gréat is the glóry of the Lórd!'

The Lord is hígh yet he lóoks on the lówly
and the haúghty he knóws from afár.
Though I wálk in the mídst of afflíction
you give me lífe and frustráte my fóes.

You strétch out your hánd and sáve me,
your hánd will do áll things for mé.
Your lóve, O Lórd, is etérnal,
discárd not the wórk of your hánds.

Ant. Before the angels I will bless you, my God.
Ant. 2: Out of the depths I cry to you, O Lord.

Out of the depths I cry

Psalm 129 (130)

He will save his people from their sins (Mt 1:21)

Out of the dépths I crý to you, O Lórd,
Lórd, hear my vóice!
O lét your éars be atténtive
to the vóice of my pléading.

If you, O Lórd, should márk our gúilt,
Lórd, who would survíve?
But with yóu is fóund forgíveness:
for thís we revére you.

My sóul is wáiting for the Lórd,
I cóunt on his wórd.
My sóul is lónging for the Lórd
more than wátchman for dáybreak.
Let the wátchman cóunt on dáybreak
and Ísrael on the Lórd.

Becáuse with the Lórd there is mércy
and fúlness of redémption,
Ísrael indéed he will redéem
from áll its iníquity.

Ant. Out of the depths I cry to you, O Lord.

WEEK 4: TUESDAY

SCRIPTURE READING   Col 3:16

Christ's message, in all its richness, must live in your hearts. Teach and instruct each other with all wisdom. Sing psalms, hymns, and sacred songs; sing to God, with thanksgiving in your hearts.

SHORT RESPONSORY

℟ You will give me the fulness of joy in your presence, O Lord.
℣ I will find happiness at your right hand for ever.

INTERCESSIONS

Christ taught us to set our hearts on the Kingdom of God, and on its justice. In that Kingdom all that we need will be given to us. Until then, let us pray: ℟ Your Kingdom come, O Lord.

Blessed are those who know their need of God: – lead us to seek your face in purity of heart. ℟

Blessed are those who work for no reward, those who suffer for what is right: – comfort them with your presence, lighten their burden. ℟

Blessed are the gentle, those who show mercy, and forgive; – they shall know your forgiveness at the end of time. ℟

Blessed are the peacemakers, those who reconcile conflict and hate: – they are indeed the sons of God. ℟

Bring consolation to all who mourn the dead: – may they share the blessed hope of all who have died in the peace of Christ. ℟

Our Father

Week 4: Wednesday

MORNING PRAYER

PSALMODY
Ant. I will praise my God all my days.

**The happiness of those
who put their trust in the Lord** Psalm 145 (146)

Let us praise the Lord all our days, that is, in all our conduct (Arnobius)

> My sóul, give práise to the Lórd;
> I will práise the Lórd all my dáys,
> make músic to my Gód while I líve.
>
> Pút no trúst in prínces,
> in mortal mén in whóm there is no hélp.
> Take their bréath, they retúrn to cláy
> and their pláns that dáy come to nóthing.
>
> He is háppy who is hélped by Jacob's Gód,
> whose hópe is in the Lórd his Gód,
> who alóne made héaven and éarth,
> the séas and áll they contáin.
>
> It is hé who keeps fáith for éver,
> who is júst to thóse who are oppréssed.
> It is hé who gives bréad to the húngry,
> the Lórd, who sets prísoners frée,

WEEK 4: WEDNESDAY

> the Lórd who gives síght to the blínd,
> whoráises up thóse who are bowed dówn,
> the Lórd, who protécts the stránger
> and uphólds the wídow and órphan.
>
> It is the Lórd who lóves the júst
> but thwárts the páth of the wícked.
> The Lórd will réign for éver,
> Sion's Gód, from áge to áge.

Ant. I will praise my God all my days.

SCRIPTURE READING Deut 4:39–40a
Understand this today and take it to heart: the Lord is God indeed, in heaven above as on earth beneath, he and no other. Keep his laws and commandments as I give them to you today.

SHORT RESPONSORY
℟ I will praise the Lord at all times.
℣ His praise will be always on my lips.

INTERCESSIONS
Praise be to the God and Father of our Lord Jesus Christ. In his great mercy, he gave us new birth into a living hope by his Son's resurrection from the dead. To him we pray: ℟ Father, give us your strength.
Turn our eyes to Jesus Christ your Son. – May he lead us in our faith and bring it to perfection. ℟
We pray for cheerfulness and a generous heart; – may we bring joy to our homes, to our work, and to all whom we meet. ℟
We pray for all who are working today; – be with them at home and in the city, in the factory and in the fields. ℟
We pray for those who have no work; – we pray for the disabled and the sick, for those who cannot find work, and for those who are retired. ℟
Our Father

WEEK 4: WEDNESDAY

EVENING PRAYER

PSALMODY
Ant. How wonderful is this knowledge of yours that you have shown me, Lord.

The Lord sees all things Psalm 138 (139):1–18, 23–24

Who could ever know the mind of the Lord? Who could ever be his counsellor? (Rom 11:34)

I

O Lórd, you séarch me and you knów me,
you knów my résting and my rísing,
you discérn my púrpose from afár.
You márk when I wálk or lie dówn,
all my wáys lie ópen to yóu.

Before éver a wórd is on my tóngue
you knów it, O Lórd, through and thróugh.
Behínd and befóre you besíege me,
your hánd ever láid upón me.
Too wónderful for mé, this knówledge,
too hígh, beyónd my réach.

O whére can I gó from your spírit,
or whére can I flée from your fáce?
If I clímb the héavens, you are thére.
If I líe in the gráve, you are thére.

If I táke the wíngs of the dáwn
and dwéll at the séa's furthest énd,
even thére your hánd would léad me,
your ríght hand would hóld me fást.

135

WEEK 4: WEDNESDAY

If I sáy: 'Let the dárkness híde me
and the líght aróund me be níght,'
even dárkness is not dárk for yóu
and the níght is as cléar as the dáy.

Ant. How wonderful is this knowledge of yours that you have shown me, Lord.
Ant. 2: I am the Lord, who test the mind and heart; I give each man what his conduct deserves.

II
For it was yóu who créated my béing,
knit me togéther in my móther's wómb.
I thánk you for the wónder of my béing,
for the wónders of áll your creátion.

Alréady you knéw my sóul,
my bódy held no sécret from yóu
when Í was being fáshioned in sécret
and móulded in the dépths of the éarth.

Your éyes saw áll my áctions,
they were áll of them wrítten in your bóok;
every óne of my dáys was decréed
before óne of them cáme into béing.

To mé, how mystérious your thóughts,
the súm of them nót to be númbered!
If I cóunt them, they are móre than the sánd;
to fínish, I must be etérnal, like yóu.

O séarch me, Gód, and know my héart.
O tést me and knów my thóughts.
See that I fóllow not the wróng páth
and léad me in the páth of life etérnal.

WEEK 4: WEDNESDAY

Ant. I am the Lord, who test the mind and heart; I give each man what his conduct deserves.

SCRIPTURE READING   1 Jn 2:3–6

We can be sure that we know God
only by keeping his commandments.
Anyone who says, 'I know him',
and does not keep his commandments,
is a liar,
refusing to admit the truth.
But when anyone does obey what he has said,
God's love comes to perfection in him.
We can be sure that we are in God
only when the one who claims to be living in him
is living the same kind of life as Christ lived.

SHORT RESPONSORY
℟ Guard us, Lord, as the apple of your eye.
℣ Hide us in the shadow of your wings.

INTERCESSIONS
Let us ask the Father, from whom every family in heaven and on earth takes its name, to send the Spirit of his Son into our hearts as we pray: ℟ Lord, in your mercy, hear our prayer.
O Lord, the creator and redeemer of all mankind, we humbly pray for all men of every race in every kind of need: – make your ways known to them, and reveal your salvation to all nations. ℟
May the whole Church be guided and governed by your Holy Spirit; – let all who call themselves Christians be led into the way of truth and hold the faith in unity of spirit. ℟
We commend to your fatherly goodness all who are afflicted or distressed; – comfort and relieve them according to their needs, and grant them the love and consolation of your Spirit. ℟

WEEK 4: WEDNESDAY

Father, give a place of life and rest to those who have died in your peace: – may we share with them in the glory of Jesus Christ, who died to save us all. R̷
Our Father

Week 4: Thursday

MORNING PRAYER

PSALMODY
Ant. In the morning let me know your love, O Lord.

Prayer in desolation Psalm 142 (143):1–11

A man is made righteous not by obedience to the Law, but by faith in Jesus Christ (Gal 2:16)

Lórd, lísten to my práyer:
túrn your éar to my appéal.
You are fáithful, you are júst; give ánswer.
Do not cáll your sérvant to júdgment
for nó one is júst in your síght.

The énemy pursúes my sóul;
he has crúshed my lífe to the gróund;
he has máde me dwéll in dárkness
like the déad, lóng forgótten.
Thérefore my spírit fáils;
my héart is númb withín me.

I remémber the dáys that are pást:
I pónder áll your wórks.
I múse on what your hánd has wróught
and to yóu I strétch out my hánds.
Like a párched land my sóul thirsts for yóu.

Lórd, make háste and ánswer;
for my spírit fáils withín me.

WEEK 4: THURSDAY

Dó not híde your fáce
lest I becóme like thóse in the gráve.

In the mórning let me knów your lóve
for I pút my trúst in yóu.
Make me knów the wáy I should wálk:
to yóu I líft up my sóul.

Réscue me, Lórd, from my énemies;
I have fléd to yóu for réfuge.
Téach me to dó your wíll
for yóu, O Lórd, are my Gód.
Let yóur good spírit guíde me
in wáys that are lével and smóoth.

For your náme's sake, Lórd, save my lífe;
in your jústice save my sóul from distréss.

Ant. In the morning let me know your love, O Lord.

SCRIPTURE READING   Rom 8:18–21
I consider that the sufferings of this present time are not worth comparing with the glory that is to be revealed to us. For the creation waits with eager longing for the revealing of the sons of God; for the creation was subjected to futility, not of its own will but by the will of him who subjected it in hope; because the creation itself will be set free from its bondage to decay and obtain the glorious liberty of the children of God.

SHORT RESPONSORY
℞ Early in the morning I will think of you, O Lord.
℣ You have been my help.

INTERCESSIONS
It is the Father's will that men should see him in the face of his beloved Son. Let us honour him as we say: ℞ Hallowed be your name.

WEEK 4: THURSDAY

Christ greeted us with good news: – may the world hear it through us, and find hope. ℟

We praise and thank you, Lord of heaven and earth; – you are the hope and joy of men in every age. ℟

May Christ's coming transform the Church; – and renew its youth and vigour in the service of men. ℟

We pray for Christians who suffer for their belief: – sustain them in their hope. ℟

Our Father

EVENING PRAYER

PSALMODY
Ant. Sion, praise your God, who has sent out his word to the earth.

The renewal of Jerusalem Psalm 147

Come, and I will show you the bride that the Lamb has married (Rev 21:9)

O práise the Lórd, Jerúsalem!
Síon, práise your Gód!

He has stréngthened the bárs of your gátes,
he has bléssed the chíldren withín you.
He estáblished péace on your bórders,
he féeds you with fínest whéat.

He sénds out his wórd to the éarth
and swíftly rúns his commánd.
He shówers down snów white as wóol,
he scátters hóar-frost like áshes.

He húrls down háilstones like crúmbs.
The wáters are frózen at his tóuch;

WEEK 4: THURSDAY

he sénds forth his wórd and it mélts them:
at the bréath of his móuth the waters flów.

He mákes his wórd known to Jácob,
to Ísrael his láws and decrées.
He has not déalt thus with óther nátions;
he has not táught them hís decrées.

Ant. Sion, praise your God, who has sent out his word to the earth.
Ant. Victory and empire have now been won by our God.

The judgment of God   Canticle: Rev 11:17–18; 12:10b–12a

We give thanks to you, Lord God Almighty,
who are and who were,
that you have taken your great power
and begun to reign.

The nations raged,
but your wrath came,
and the time for the dead to be judged,
for rewarding your servants, the prophets and saints,
and those who fear your name,
both small and great.

Now the salvation and the power
and the kingdom of our God
and the authority of his Christ have come,
for the accuser of our brethren has been thrown down,
who accuses them day and night before our God.

And they have conquered him
by the blood of the Lamb
and by the word of their testimony,
for they loved not their lives even unto death.
Rejoice, then, O heaven,
and you that dwell therein.

WEEK 4: THURSDAY

Ant. Victory and empire have now been won by our God.

SCRIPTURE READING   Cf Col 1:23
You must, of course, continue faithful on a sure and firm foundation, and not allow yourselves to be shaken from the hope you gained when you heard the gospel which has been preached to everybody in the world.

SHORT RESPONSORY
℟ The Lord is my shepherd; there is nothing I shall want.
℣ Fresh and green are the pastures where he gives me repose.

INTERCESSIONS
The light shines out in the darkness and the darkness cannot overcome it. Let us thank our Lord for bringing his light to our lives. ℟ Lord Jesus Christ, you are our light.
Word of God, you have brought the light of eternity to the darkened world: – may it open the minds and hearts of all the children of the Church. ℟
Show your care for all who dedicate their lives to the service of others: – may your grace inspire their actions and sustain them to the end. ℟
Lord, you healed the paralytic and forgave him his sins: – pardon all our guilt, and heal the wounds of our sins. ℟
Men follow the light to new knowledge and discovery: – may they use your gifts to serve the whole human family, and so give glory to you. ℟
Lead the dead from darkness into your own wonderful light; – in your mercy show them the radiance of your glory. ℟
Our Father

Week 4: Friday

MORNING PRAYER

PSALMODY
Ant. My food is to do the will of my Father.

Thanksgiving and request for help
Psalm 39 (40):2–14, 17–18

You wanted no sacrifice or oblation, but you have prepared a body for me (Heb 10:5)

I wáited, I wáited for the Lórd
and he stóoped down to mé;
he héard my crý.

He dréw me from the déadly pít,
from the míry cláy.
He sét my féet upon a róck
and made my fóotsteps fírm.

He pút a new sóng into my móuth,
práise of our Gód.
Mány shall sée and féar
and shall trúst in the Lórd.

Háppy the mán who has pláced
his trúst in the Lórd
and has nót gone óver to the rébels
who fóllow false góds.

How mány, O Lórd my Gód,
are the wónders and desígns

that yóu have wórked for ús;
you háve no équal.

Shóuld I procláim and spéak of them,
they are móre than I can téll!

You do not ásk for sácrifice and ófferings,
but an ópen éar.
You do not ask for hólocaust and víctim.
Instéad, here am Í.

In the scroll of the bóok it stands wrítten
that Í should do your wíll.
My Gód, I delíght in your láw.
in the dépth of my héart.

Your jústice Í have procláimed
in the gréat assémbly.
My líps I háve not séaled;
you knów it, O Lórd.

I have not hídden your jústice in my héart
but decláred your faithful hélp.
I have not hídden your lóve and your trúth
from the gréat assémbly.

O Lórd, you wíll not withhóld
your compássion from me.
Your mérciful lóve and your trúth
will álways guárd me.

For Í am besét with évils
too mány to be cóunted.
My síns have fállen upón me
and my síght fáils me.
They are móre than the háirs of my héad
and my héart sínks.

WEEK 4: FRIDAY

O Lórd, cóme to my réscue,
Lord, cóme to my áid.

O lét there be rejóicing and gládness
for áll who séek you.
Let them éver say: 'The Lórd is gréat',
who lóve your saving hélp.

As for mé, wrétched and póor,
the Lórd thinks of mé,
Yóu are my réscuer, my hélp,
O Gód, do not déláy.

Ant. My food is to do the will of my Father.

SCRIPTURE READING   Gal 2:19b–20
With Christ I hang upon the cross, and yet I am alive; or rather, not I; it is Christ that lives in me. True, I am living, here and now, this mortal life; but my real life is the faith I have in the Son of God, who loved me, and gave himself for me.

SHORT RESPONSORY
℟ I call to the Lord, the Most High, for he has been my help.
℣ May he send from heaven and save me.

INTERCESSIONS
Christ is the image of the unseen God, the first-born of all creation, and the first to be born from the dead. All things are to be reconciled through him because he made peace by his death on the cross. We pray to him: ℟ Lord Jesus, come to us today.
We have been baptized into your death: – may we be cleansed of greed and envy, and clothed in the strength and gentleness of your love. ℟
We have been sealed with the Holy Spirit who has been given to us; – confirm us in your service, and help us to bear witness to you in the society in which we live. ℟

WEEK 4: FRIDAY

Before you suffered, you longed to eat the passover with your disciples: – as we take part in your eucharist, may we share in your resurrection. ℟
You continue to work in your faithful people: – create through them a new world where injustice and destruction will give way to growth, freedom and hope. ℟
Our Father

EVENING PRAYER

PSALMODY
Ant. I will bless you day after day and tell of your wonderful deeds, O Lord.

Praise of God's majesty Psalm 144 (145)

You, O Lord, are the One who was and who is, the Just One (Rev 16:5)

I will give you glóry, O Gód my Kíng,
I will bléss your náme for éver.

I will bléss you dáy after dáy
and práise your náme for éver.
The Lord is gréat, híghly to be práised,
his gréatness cánnot be méasured.

Age to áge shall procláim your wórks,
shall decláre your míghty déeds,
shall spéak of your spléndour and glóry,
tell the tále of your wónderful wórks.

They will spéak of your térrible déeds,
recóunt your gréatness and míght.
They will recáll your abúndant góodness;
age to áge shall ríng out your jústice.

WEEK 4: FRIDAY

The Lord is kínd and fúll of compássion,
slow to ánger, abóunding in lóve.
How góod is the Lord to áll,
compássionate to áll his créatures.

The Lord is fáithful in áll his wórds
and lóving in áll his déeds.
The Lórd supports all who fáll
and ráises áll who are bowed dówn.

The éyes of all créatures look to yóu
and you gíve them their fóod in due tíme.
You ópen wíde your hánd,
grant the desíres of áll who líve.

The Lord is júst in áll his wáys,
and lóving in áll his déeds.
He is clóse to áll who cáll him,
who cáll on hím from their héarts.

He gránts the desíres of those who féar him,
he héars their crý and he sáves them.
The Lórd protécts all who lóve him;
but the wícked he will útterly destróy.

Let me spéak the práise of the Lórd,
let all mankínd bléss his holy náme
for éver, for áges unénding.

All your créatures shall thánk you, O Lórd,
and your fríends shall repéat their bléssing.
They shall spéak of the glóry of your réign
and decláre your míght, O Gód,

to make knówn to mén your mighty déeds
and the glórious spléndour of your réign.
Yóurs is an éverlasting kíngdom;
your rúle lasts from áge to áge.

148

WEEK 4: FRIDAY

Ant. The eyes of all creatures look to you, Lord; you are close to all who call upon you.

SCRIPTURE READING   Rom 8:1–2
There is now no condemnation for those who are in Christ Jesus. For the law of the Spirit of life in Christ Jesus has set me free from the law of sin and death.

SHORT RESPONSORY
℟ Christ died for our sins, that he might offer us to God.
℣ In the body he was put to death, in the spirit he was raised to life.

INTERCESSIONS
God's love for us was revealed when God sent into the world his only Son so that we might have life through him. We are able to love God because he loved us first. And so we pray: ℟ Lord, help us to love you and to love one another.

Jesus forgave the penitent woman her sins because she had loved much: – may we too know his healing touch and love you with all our hearts. ℟

You look with compassion on the humble and contrite of heart: – in your goodness, turn our hearts to you and help us to do what we know to be right. ℟

We acknowledge the suffering we have caused to others: – we ask forgiveness for our neglect and indifference. ℟

We ask you to remember tonight those who are in great difficulty: – give new heart to those who have lost their faith in man and in God, to those who seek the truth but cannot find it. ℟

Remember all those who put their hope in you while they lived: – through the passion and death of your Son, grant them the remission of all their sins. ℟

Our Father

Week 4: Saturday

MORNING PRAYER

PSALMODY
Ant. 1: It is good to make music to your name, O Most High, to proclaim your love in the morning.

Praise of the Lord, Creator Psalm 91 (92)

The deeds of God's only Son are praised (St Athanasius)

It is góod to give thánks to the Lórd
to make músic to your náme, O Most Hígh,
to procláim your lóve in the mórning
and your trúth in the wátches of the níght,
on the tén-stringed lýre and the lúte,
with the múrmuring sóund of the hárp.

Your déeds, O Lórd, have made me glád;
for the wórk of your hánds I shout with jóy.
O Lórd, how gréat are your wórks!
How déep are yóur desígns!
The fóolish man cánnot knów this
and the fóol cánnot understánd.

Though the wícked spring úp like gráss
and áll who do évil thríve,
they are dóomed to be etérnally destróyed.
But yóu, Lord, are etérnally on hígh.
Sée how your énemies pérish;
all dóers of évil are scáttered.

WEEK 4: SATURDAY

To mé you give the wíld-ox's stréngth;
you anóint me with the púrest óil.
My éyes looked in tríumph on my fóes;
my éars heard gládly of their fáll.
The júst will flóurish like the pálm-tree
and grów like a Lébanon cédar.

Plánted in the hóuse of the Lórd
they will flóurish in the cóurts of our Gód,
stíll bearing frúit when they are óld,
stíll full of sáp, still gréen,
to procláim that the Lórd is júst.
In hím, my róck, there is no wróng.

Ant. It is good to make music to your name, O Most High, to proclaim your love in the morning.
Ant. 2: I will give you a new heart, and put a new spirit in you.

The Lord will give his people new life

Canticle: Ezek 36:24–28

They shall be his people, and he will be their God; his name is God-with-them (Rev 21:3)

I will take you from the nations,
and gather you from all the countries,
and bring you into your own land.

I will sprinkle clean water upon you,
and you shall be clean from all your uncleannesses,
and from all your idols I will cleanse you.

A new heart I will give you,
and a new spirit I will put within you;
and I will take out of your flesh the heart of stone
and give you a heart of flesh.

WEEK 4: SATURDAY

And I will put my spirit within you,
and cause you to walk in my statutes
and be careful to observe my ordinances.

You shall dwell in the land
which I gave to your fathers;
and you shall be my people,
and I will be your God.

Ant. I will give you a new heart, and put a new spirit in you.

SCRIPTURE READING 2 Pet 3:13–14
What we are waiting for is what he promised: the new heavens and the new earth, the place where righteousness will be at home. So then, my friends, while you are waiting, do your best to live lives without spot or stain so that he will find you at peace. Think of our Lord's patience as your opportunity to be saved.

SHORT REPSONSORY
℟ When I sing to you my lips shall rejoice.
℣ My tongue shall tell the tale of your justice.

INTERCESSIONS
God's gift was not a spirit of timidity, but the Spirit of power, and love, and self-control. With complete confidence we pray: ℟ Father, send us your Spirit.
Praise be to God, the Father of our Lord Jesus Christ: – in Christ you have given us every spiritual blessing. ℟
By the power of the Holy Spirit, Mary brought Christ into the world: – through the Church, may Christ be born again today in the hearts of men. ℟
Father, may your Spirit lead us forward out of solitude: – may he lead us to open the eyes of the blind, to proclaim the Word of light, to reap together the harvest of life. ℟

WEEK 4: SATURDAY

Let our striving for your kingdom not fall short through selfishness or fear: – may the universe be alive with the Spirit, and our homes be the pledge of a world redeemed. ℟
Our Father

EVENING PRAYER

PSALMODY
Ant. Come before the Lord, singing for joy.

The joy of those who enter the temple of the Lord

Psalm 99 (100)

The Lord calls all those he has redeemed to sing a hymn of victory (St Athanasius)

Cry out with jóy to the Lórd, all the éarth.
Sérve the Lórd with gládness.
Come befóre him, sínging for jóy.

Know that hé, the Lórd, is Gód.
He máde us, we belóng to hím,
we are his péople, the shéep of his flóck.

Gó within his gátes, giving thánks.
Enter his cóurts with sóngs of práise.
Give thánks to him and bléss his náme.

Indéed, how góod is the Lórd,
etérnal his mérciful lóve.
He is fáithful from áge to áge.

Ant. Come before the Lord, singing for joy.
Ant. The Lord Jesus humbled himself; therefore God has highly exalted him for ever.

WEEK 4: SATURDAY

Christ, the servant of God Canticle: Phil 2:6–11

Though he was in the form of God,
Jesus did not count equality with God a thing to be grasped.

He emptied himself,
taking the form of a servant,
being born in the likeness of men.

And being found in human form,
he humbled himself and became obedient unto death,
even death on a cross.

Therefore God has highly exalted him
and bestowed on him the name which is above every name,

That at the name of Jesus every knee should bow,
in heaven and on earth and under the earth,

And every tongue confess that Jesus Christ is Lord,
to the glory of God the Father.

Ant. The Lord Jesus humbled himself; therefore God has highly exalted him for ever.

SCRIPTURE READING Rom 11:33–36

How great are God's riches! How deep are his wisdom and knowledge! Who can explain his decisions? Who can understand his ways? As the scripture says, 'Who knows the mind of the Lord? Who is able to give him advice? Who has ever given him anything, so that he had to pay it back?' For all things were created by him, and all things exist through him and for him. To God be glory forever! Amen.

SHORT RESPONSORY

℟ How great are your works, O Lord.
℣ In wisdom you have made them all.

WEEK 4: SATURDAY

INTERCESSIONS

Glory be to the one God, Father, Son, and Holy Spirit as we humbly pray: ℟ Lord, be with your people.

Almighty Father, bring justice to our world, – that your people may live in the joy of your peace. ℟

Bring all peoples into your kingdom, – that all mankind may be saved. ℟

Give to married people the strength of your peace, the guidance of your will, – and the grace to live together in constant love. ℟

Be the reward of all who have given us their help, – and grant them eternal life. ℟

Have mercy on those who have lost their lives through warfare or violence, – and receive them into your rest. ℟

Our Father

THE LORD'S PRAYER

Our Father, who art in heaven,
hallowed be thy name,
Thy kingdom come,
Thy will be done on earth, as it is in heaven.
Give us this day our daily bread,
and forgive us our trespasses,
as we forgive those who trespass against us
and lead us not into temptation,
but deliver us from evil.

For thine is the kingdom, the power and the glory,
Now and forever,

Amen.